'A pioneer in her field, the Revd Pam ~~...~~ guide to the theological and practical concerns of online worship, fellowship and spiritual direction. From first-hand experience, she gives the reader both a theological rationale and practical wisdom for conducting online ministry. Examples of liturgy for "virtual" services, guidelines for creating safe online community and principles for online team ministry are all included in this helpful book. Highly recommended!'

Maggi Dawn, Associate Professor of Theology
and Literature, Yale Divinity School

'Pam Smith has an enthusiasm for sharing the gospel of God rather than worshipping technology. She challenges those who fear online ministry, both theologically and with practical advice, identifying opportunities *and* areas that need respectful thought. In order to meet people where they are – online – Pam emphasizes the need for resilience in our own Christian development, and highlights quality interactions over quantity. I recommend it to all who are interested in or involved in online mission and ministry.'

Dr Bex Lewis, Research Fellow in Social Media and Online
Learning, The CODEC Research Centre for Digital Theology

'If it is serious about ministry and mission the Church needs to be present in each culture's conversation spaces, listening with care, learning with humility and speaking in quiet confidence. In *Online Mission and Ministry*, Pam Smith makes a compelling case for living and sharing online the great story of Jesus. The author suggests that digital space may prove to be a particularly "thin place" in which the Christ is encountered through conversation, participation and community. Insightful, practical and inspiring!'

Ian Adams, poet, writer and digital creative author
of Unfurling, and creator of Morning Bell,
a digital journal and blog

'As the bishop with the pastoral responsibility for i-church, it has been a great privilege to work with Pam Smith over the years. Her book is a wonderful distillation of the wisdom she has gleaned by being at the forefront of these developments and I warmly commend it to you.'

The Rt Revd Colin Fletcher OBE, Bishop of Dorchester

'Pam Smith has been at the forefront of the critical relationship between the Church and the internet and social media in the UK, and this book shows why. Read it if you want to think and do more about social media and mission and ministry.'

The Revd Canon David Male, Director of the Centre for Pioneer Learning, Ridley Hall, Cambridge

ONLINE MISSION AND MINISTRY

ONLINE MISSION AND MINISTRY

A theological and practical guide

Pam Smith

First published in Great Britain in 2015

Society for Promoting Christian Knowledge
36 Causton Street
London SW1P 4ST
www.spckpublishing.co.uk

Copyright © Pam Smith 2015

All rights reserved. No part of this book may be reproduced or transmitted in any form
or by any means, electronic or mechanical, including photocopying, recording,
or by any information storage and retrieval system, without permission
in writing from the publisher.

SPCK does not necessarily endorse the individual views contained in its publications.

The author and publisher have made every effort to ensure that the external website
and email addresses included in this book are correct and up to date at the time
of going to press. The author and publisher are not responsible for
the content, quality or continuing accessibility of the sites.

Unless otherwise noted, Scripture quotations are taken from the New Revised Standard
Version of the Bible, Anglicized Edition, copyright © 1989, 1995 by the Division of
Christian Education of the National Council of the Churches of Christ in
the USA. Used by permission. All rights reserved.

British Library Cataloguing-in-Publication Data
A catalogue record for this book is available from the British Library

ISBN 978–0–281–07151–7
eBook ISBN 978–0–281–07152–4

Typeset by Graphicraft Limited, Hong Kong
First printed in Great Britain by Ashford Colour Press
Subsequently digitally printed in Great Britain

eBook by Graphicraft Limited, Hong Kong

Produced on paper from sustainable forests

Contents

Acknowledgements   viii

Introduction   ix

1   Techno Christianity   1

2   Theological understandings   11

3   Where do I start?   26

4   Pastoral care and relationships   41

5   Online discipleship and spirituality   55

6   Dealing with difficult and disruptive people   70

7   Building an online community   87

8   Looking after yourself and your team   102

Appendix 1: Example of a worship and prayer service
for a chat room   116

Appendix 2: Sample forum rules   119

Appendix 3: Further reading   122

Appendix 4: Useful websites   123

Notes   124

Acknowledgements

Enormous thanks are due to my husband Jim, who has supported my ministry in every way possible over the last ten years, to my sons Sam and Chris and daughter-in-law Sarah for their love and encouragement, and to Gill and Di for cheering me on.

My ideas about online mission and ministry have been worked out by reflection with others, particularly within the i-church community. I am especially grateful to my i-church colleagues Caroline Birchmore, Karen Wellman and Jae Raddon, whose insights have contributed an enormous amount to my understanding.

Great thanks are also due to Bex Lewis for her support and encouragement, to Bishop Colin Fletcher, who has been the 'i-church bishop' for the past ten years, to the Diocese of Oxford for its support, to Simon Jenkins and Steve Goddard, the founders of the Ship of Fools website, for their vision and commitment to online Christianity, and to all my online friends from whom I have learnt so much. You know who you are :-)

Last, I would like to thank my editor Tracey Messenger for her patient support, coaching, helpful suggestions and her belief in me. I certainly could not have written this book without her.

Introduction

In 2004 two online churches started in the UK, the Church of Fools and i-church. They were considered so unusual that they both attracted headlines all over the world and hundreds of potential members had to be turned away.

While that level of novelty has worn off, people still do a double take when I tell them that I am the priest in charge of an online church. After the double take come the inevitable questions, often deserving of a much longer and better thought-out answer than I am able to give on the spur of the moment. This book is my attempt to answer to all those questions in the depth they deserve.

There are no 'experts' in online ministry – it is a field where practitioners need to keep learning all the time. This book therefore is not a 'How to . . .' manual, but more an encouragement to those who are interested to dip their toe in the water. It should also be useful to anyone who is already involved in online mission and ministry, to those in decision-making roles who are involved in supporting or resourcing someone else who is involved, and to theological and religious studies students who want to look at online ministry.

I hope you will learn as much from reading the book as I have learnt from writing it.

1

Techno Christianity

In the beginning . . .

I started to go online in the 1990s, shortly after the world wide web became available to people with home computers. I was teaching in a college which had a suite of computers connected to the internet, and having tried it out there I bought a modem and went online at home. Home internet connections worked on a 'dial up' basis in those days, and there was quite a long pause after clicking to go online while the modem dialled, and then connected to, distant telephone exchanges. The noise of the dialling tones gave the impression of travelling a long distance to reach the mysterious place called 'cyber space' where I could read what other people had posted on the world wide web. I didn't realize at first that it was possible to 'chat' to people online in real time, and the first time someone started up a live chat with me I experienced the same sort of shock as I might have had if a character in a book had started speaking to me. A text box suddenly popped up on to my screen and someone in the USA started typing questions about where I lived and why I was looking at that particular web page. At first this live interaction made me feel very nervous, but I soon started to feel more comfortable about 'chatting' to people I couldn't see.

In these early days, connecting to the internet from a home computer required the exclusive use of a phone line, so if I was online nobody else in the house could make or receive a phone call. Most internet service providers (ISPs) charged by the minute for being online. The time I was online cost a significant amount of money and cut the rest of the household off from telephone contact with the outside world.

Despite these limitations, I quickly became enthusiastic about being able to 'meet' and talk to people online. I had only been a Christian for a few years, and I found the opportunity to discuss Christianity with people from different backgrounds and at different stages in their faith journey helped me to develop my own faith. One website, the Ship of Fools,[1] subtitled 'The magazine of Christian unrest', hosted discussion forums where people from a wide range of backgrounds debated the Christian faith and its place in contemporary society. The Ship, as it was known to its users, had a tradition of arranging offline meetings between members, and when I visited my brother in the USA, several American members arranged to travel to meet me with my family in Washington for a meal and a trip to the zoo. Meeting people who had previously only been known to me through online conversations was an odd experience at first – the mental images I had formed didn't always fit the faces of the people I saw in front of me. After a few minutes, however, the person I 'knew' from talking to him or her online merged with the person in front of me, adding another dimension to relationships which had originally started through exchanging words on a screen.

Knowing people online, and occasionally meeting up with them, became so commonplace to me that I didn't realize I was somewhat ahead of the curve, particularly in church culture. A couple of months after I met up with Ship of Fools friends in Washington, DC, I went on an away day with the church council, having just been voted on as a member. As an ice breaker, we were told to exchange with the person next to us 'an unusual fact about yourself', which was then to be shared with the group. I told the person next to me that when I had recently visited my brother in the United States, I had met up with some people I had first encountered online. His face froze into a horrified expression as he struggled to find something to say. If I had told him that I had broken into a house and stolen someone's jewellery, I don't think he could have looked much more shocked. This was my first realization that use of 'new' technology in church might provoke suspicion rather than interest.

As I became increasingly involved in mission and ministry in my local church, I started to feel that the internet could be used in mission. The same thing obviously occurred to other Christians, and a number of intentionally missionary online projects were started.[2] In 2004, I was given the opportunity to join the team of the Church of Fools,[3] an experimental online church started by the Ship of Fools management, while I was training for ordained ministry. Four years later, at the end of my curacy (training post), I was appointed as priest in charge of i-church.[4]

The Christians I knew who were engaged in these and similar projects saw the internet as a new territory – **cyber space** or **virtual reality** – and believed that Christians should establish a presence there, just as missionaries had always travelled to proclaim the gospel in new lands. However, there was a reluctance among many members of mainstream churches to become involved. Although people were increasingly using the internet in their workplaces and homes, churches remained internet-free zones for quite a long time. It sometimes felt as if churches wanted to protect their members from technological change. In the last ten years, mobile and digital technology have become commonplace in the home and in the workplace, yet it is still the case that many churches are reluctant to engage with this 'new' technology, even if ministers and many of the members use mobile phones and computers in their everyday lives. It is as if the Church wants to exist outside the digitized society around it, standing firm against the rising tide of technological innovation, forgetting that the Church and the

Christian faith have previously been shaped and reshaped by technology.

It is, of course, inaccurate to characterize all churches as resistant to change – some churches readily adopt new technology, including digital technology, to equip themselves for worship and mission. However, some church communities are suspicious, or even fearful, of change and will hang on to 'the old way of doing things', whether it is old hymn books, the same set pattern of services or outdated equipment. Such communities may be resistant to the notion that they have to adopt a completely new form of communication and go online to make disciples.

Technology – opportunity or threat?

Despite its origins being traceable to the early seventeenth century,[5] the word 'technology' has in the last 50 or so years gained a progressive, even futuristic, ring, being associated with ideas and processes which will drive society forward. In the abstract for his paper 'Technik comes to America: changing meanings of technology before 1930', Eric Schatzberg describes how the word 'technology' acquired its current meaning:

> In German-speaking regions, a new discourse emerged around *die Technik* in the second half of the nineteenth century. This German term referred to the practical arts as a whole, especially those associated with engineers and modern industry. When Thorstein Veblen encountered this term after 1900 in German social theory, he incorporated its meanings into technology, thereby transforming the English word into a sophisticated concept for analyzing industrial societies. Most scholars who drew on Veblen's concept missed its subtleties, however, among them the historian Charles A. Beard. In the late 1920s, Beard embraced a deterministic understanding of technology that linked it firmly to the idea of progress.[6]

Phrases such as 'the white heat of technology', attributed to Labour Party leader Harold Wilson in 1963, increased the sense of a technological revolution that would create a new kind of society. This included the widening use of computers in manufacturing and science.[7] The phrase 'information technology' – usually shortened to IT – became synonymous with the introduction of computers into the workplace, and computers and the information they contained were seen as instruments of progress and change.[8] Networks of computers were developed to share information among academics and scientists, and from this the world wide web was created, where information could be made available via larger computers called servers to anyone whose computer joined the network.

As Christians and as churches, we need to understand how communication is changing and adapt the way we communicate both within church and with those we wish to reach with the gospel. We must avoid reaching the point where what we do inside the church is so distant from what we do in our homes and workplaces that people assume our gospel is as outmoded as our technology. If we insist on communicating only in ways that we find familiar, we will find that fewer and fewer people are willing to listen.

'Online church? How do you do that?'

The question I am most frequently asked when I tell people that I am part of an online Christian community is 'How do you do that?' The focus of every online Christian community in which I have been involved has been on Christian mission and ministry, not on being in community for its own sake. A theologically correct answer to 'How do you do church online?' might be 'By the grace of God and in the fellowship of the Holy Spirit, in common with all Christian communities', but in addition to sounding pious and impractical, it doesn't tell people what they really want to know. I have realized that what underlies the question 'How do you do that?' is something less theological and more practical. What people really want to know is: how can people be in community with each other if they are not physically proximate to each other?

Underlying the question 'How do you do online Christian community?' is a belief that gathering together physically for worship, including Communion, is what makes a group of Christians into a community. To Christians, the word 'church' means both the people who make up a Christian community and a building in which they meet. When people with no experience of churchgoing imagine 'church', they imagine a building with people in it. The idea that a church is primarily a physical place makes it hard to imagine a church with no physical presence, made up of people who meet online, via the internet, not together in a building. Some forms of online church address this conceptual difficulty by representing a church building on screen and using 'churchy' language, but the underlying difficulty remains – if you stay in the same place physically when you are connected with other members via the internet, how can you be 'in church' as well? Chapter 4 on pastoral care and relationships, and Chapter 5 on discipleship and spirituality should give some idea about how relationships within online Christian communities work so that their members experience them as church.

The medium is the message?

Christianity is fundamentally a communication event.
                                                    (Shane Hipps)

In his book *Flickering Pixels*,[9] Shane Hipps examines the dynamic relationship between technology and the Christian message. His subtitle, *How technology shapes your faith*, reflects his thesis that Christianity as we receive it has been changed by the ways in which it has been communicated to us, and will be changed again as we communicate it. He points out that we have no choice about this change, as much as we might resist it, for it is an unavoidable part of communication that messages are changed by being transmitted. Languages change and die, so that the original texts of our Scriptures are no longer easily understand-able and have to be translated by scholars, who will have to make decisions about language which favour one interpretation over another. As Hipps points out, there has been controversy about translating the Bible into vernacular languages: 'We take our countless Bible translations for granted, but this was a bitter point of contention at various points of church history. The church has a history and a habit of resisting technological changes.'[10]

Hipps believes that spreading the gospel as far as possible involves not just linguistic translation but the 'translation' of the message into new formats, concluding that this will inevitably change it: 'You can't change methods without changing your message – they're inseparable.'[11]

He uses the example of the printing press – which he calls 'an explosion of nuclear proportions'[12] – to demonstrate how technology changes things in an unpredictable way; for example, after the advent of printed Bibles, the wide open spaces in medieval churches in which people stood for worship were filled with rows of pews. In this way, the physical layout of churches started to resemble the printed columns inside a book. And, says Hipps, the influence of printing went even further:

> The values of efficiency and linear sequence, which became more entrenched in the Western world with each passing decade, changed the way the gospel was conceived. Under the force of the printed word, the gospel message was efficiently compressed into a linear sequential formula:
>
> Apologize for your sins + Believe Jesus = Go to heaven[13]

Perhaps it is the recognition, or fear, that the message may be changed which makes churches reluctant to adopt new media for transmitting the gospel.

If Shane Hipps is right, and the system of communication being used affects the gospel it is communicating, what effect will the use of social media and digital communications have on the gospel we are communicating? The ready availability of translations and Bible study tools online means anyone can have access to the sort of information only available to serious scholars a generation ago. There are tools for joint exploration of the meaning of the gospel, not just in the abstract but in the impact it has on our lives in the here and now.

Networked gospel?

The world wide web is a network of networks. When you connect to a web page you are connecting to a server – a large computer which hosts the information, or code, that your computer translates into words and pictures. The image of a web conveys the way computers are linked to each other, and also the way web pages are connected to each other by links in HTML (or Hyper Text Markup Language). Clicking on a link will take you to another page, and links on that page may take you to still more – all the pages you visit are connected directly to other pages, and indirectly by the links on those pages to many more.

Online relationships work in a similar way: when you connect with someone on a social media site, you become linked to the other people he or she is connected to by seeing the same posts by your mutual acquaintance. People may become friends online through knowing the same people, even though they have never met offline. The phrase 'six degrees of separation', which became the title of a play and a film by John Guare, describes a theory first set out by Frigyes Karinthy in 1929 that anyone in the world can be linked to anyone else in no more than six steps of 'friend of a friend' connections. It is this sense of interconnectedness that attracts some people to social networking and online relationships.

There is no system of government or leadership in a network. The world wide web is a system of networks that anyone can join. Within an environment of networked relationships, your importance grows not by occupying a hierarchical position, but because of the number of networks of which you are a part. This has implications for how authority is attained and exercised. Our awareness of networks may lead us to a different understanding of the relationships we see in the gospel and other parts of the Bible. Perhaps we will see a move away from the 'broadcast' of the correct way to interpret the Bible and into a much more discursive way of teaching and learning about our faith.

'All may; none must; some should'

Although in this book I am advocating the use of digital technology for mission and ministry, those of us who are enthusiasts for exploring new ways of communicating the gospel should bear in mind that not everyone is called to make this their primary ministry. I was told once about making confession that: 'All may; none must; some should'. This is a helpful rule of thumb to guide us in all our enthusiasms. We should be evangelists for Christ, not for a particular methodology. God has many ways to reach people and many ways in which people can reach out. This book is intended to help those who feel drawn to explore this form of mission and ministry – it does not seek to force new forms of ministry on people who do not feel called to them. We are called to spread the good news of Jesus Christ. If we find ourselves instead spreading the good news of how wonderful the internet is, we may need to take a step back and rethink our approach.

'The harvest is plentiful . . .' (Luke 10.2)

Some aspects of online mission and ministry described in this book are challenging, but the potential rewards are great.

There are no 'experts' in online mission and ministry – everyone learns by experience. If you are interested in exploring this exciting new mission field, or have already started, I hope this book will encourage you to join the labourers who are already there.

2

Theological understandings

———•◦•———

Christians who become actively involved in online ministry can usually articulate a clear sense of being called by God to mission in the context of digital space. Of course, the personal conviction of being called to a particular role does not, in itself, prove that a calling exists. Traditionally, an individual sense of calling is discerned, and ministry authorized, by the wider Church. A problem arises with a sense of calling to online ministry when the wider Church doesn't know how to test out such a calling, or even if such a calling might exist. Criticism of online ministry is often existential, in that critics do not just criticize aspects of it but refuse to accept its validity as part of God's mission at all. Some people may even state that it is detrimental to the Church.

Criticism which starts from a negative view of something about which we feel overwhelmingly positive is hard to address and can feel personally wounding. However, as practitioners of online mission and ministry, we need to be able to answer questions and explain our work in terms that are understandable to people with little or no experience of it, in order to enlist their understanding and support. This is not just a practical issue, but also an ecclesiological one. Without support from, and accountability to, the wider Church, it is arguable that online Christian groups will not function fully as part of the body of Christ. Not only will this affect online mission and ministry, it will also affect the wider Church as it will, in effect, be functioning with a part missing.

This chapter is therefore intended to enable practitioners to talk about online mission and ministry to people who may be unfamiliar with the concept, in the hope of increasing their understanding and their support. It explains how reflection might be done, and covers some of the main criticisms people make of online ministry, suggesting ways of addressing them in a reasoned and reasonable way.

Reflecting on our practice

The term 'reflective practice' is used in person-centred professions such as medicine, education and social work to describe a process whereby practitioners learn by analysing their actions and draw lessons about how to proceed in the future. Those in training for ministry learn to be reflective practitioners by undertaking a process called **theological reflection**, which enables them to learn from what they have done and improve their awareness of what God may be saying about it. All ministerial practitioners, whether formally licensed or working less formally, should reflect theologically on what they are doing, asking questions like 'Was God in this?' 'Where was God in this?' 'What felt right about this?' 'Did anything feel wrong?' This may take place in a one-to-one session with a spiritual director, work consultant or coach, within a peer group and/or by journalling or blogging. Techniques such as **critical incident analysis**[1] and **action learning sets**[2] can be used to help us identify and analyse situations that are troubling us, enabling us to learn from them and to see the way ahead in a new light.

When we learn in this way from our lived experience, **praxis** – what we do – necessarily precedes reflection. Our reflection then feeds into our future praxis. The intention is that, over time, we will move ever nearer to being in tune with what God is calling us to do in the world.

Understanding online mission and ministry as a fresh expression of church

In the past 15 years, the Fresh Expressions movement has responded to the apparent decline in popularity of Christianity by encouraging the development of new forms of ministry at grassroots level, intended to appeal to people who are not currently being reached by traditional ministries. In answer to criticisms that this runs the risk of splitting the Church and weakening it, Fresh Expressions has made a commitment to a 'mixed economy' in which new and traditional forms of church are called to work together:

> If God's intention for the human race is that difference and oneness should be combined, should this not have implications for our understanding of church? We will hold to a vision of one transcendent united church, but positively welcome a rich variety of expressions of church locally, nationally and across the world. Francis and Richter call for a 'multiplex' church. This would allow followers of Christ to celebrate their participation in the kingdom of God in many different ways.
>
> The idea of the mixed economy seeks to make this vision real. Very diverse expressions of church would exist alongside each other in mutual fellowship. Old and new would be a blessing to one another.[3]

Like other new and experimental forms of church, online church must fit firmly into this model of mixed economy, seeking to strengthen the whole Church, not compete with existing forms.

Understanding and answering critiques of online mission and ministry

Many of the adverse reactions I have heard to online ministry appear to be rooted in an emotional rather than a thought-out response. It is difficult, if not impossible, to counter an emotional response with a logical argument. In the long run, it is more productive to keep dialogue open and maintain relationships with other Christians than to try to steamroller their misgivings with our counter-arguments. I believe the best way to answer critics is to encourage them to look closely at one or two online Christian projects and see and experience what happens there for themselves. However, if we want to motivate people to look at what we are doing, we first need to convince them there is something worth looking at.

The next section gathers together some of the most common critiques I have encountered, with some thoughts about how they might be answered. These are not intended to be used as a 'knockout punch' which will stop critics in their tracks, but to be used as part of a dialogue in which people are seeking to increase their mutual understanding.

1 'Here be dragons . . .'

When the internet first became accessible via home computers, there was a widespread expectation that this would lead to social isolation, with people staying in their houses and accessing services like shopping and education via the internet, thus eliminating the need for social interaction. Instead, the creation of the world wide web, the development of social networking sites such as Facebook and the increasing use of mobile phones for social interaction have seen a growth of interaction and connectivity rather than a reduction. Despite this, the dystopian vision of the internet as a destroyer of human interaction has persisted among a large number of Christians. People who have integrated digital communication into their everyday life are unlikely to have a moral position on it, any more than they have on the use of the telephone, but among Christians who don't habitually use the internet it may be seen as a medium which encourages moral deficiency. Most Christians would agree that Christianity should be accessible online, but think in terms of using the internet like a vast noticeboard, making information about Christianity available for people to read. The idea behind online mission and ministry is that Christians should immerse themselves in the digital world and form communities so that they can make the gospel available to others who spend time online.

Concern about the dangers of participating in online ministry may arise from a belief that the internet is a medium which can have a corrupting effect on its users. News stories about internet addiction, debts run up on pornography and gambling sites, marriages broken by extramarital affairs started in virtual worlds, and people who use the internet to abuse and terrorize others, all contribute to the impression that the internet has a corrupting and degrading effect, lowering our inhibitions and weakening our ability to resist temptation. People who are regular users of the internet may therefore be regarded as morally compromised even if they are doing it to exert a Christian influence. This may explain why some Christians are suspicious, and even antagonistic, when talking to practitioners of online mission and ministry.

If we accept that the internet can be a vehicle for temptation and a place of moral danger, should this prevent us from using it for mission? Does our calling to be 'salt and light' mean 'except in situations which challenge us'? In terms of mission and ministry, we simply can't afford to maintain the Church as a technology-free enclave if we want to find new ways of connecting with people in their everyday lives. It is not good enough to leave the digital space uncharted, with a warning 'Here be dragons' scrawled across it. Danger is no excuse – we need to put on our armour and engage.

2 *The internet diminishes our humanity*

As soon as humans started to hunt and forage for food we used agricultural tools and modified nature in order to cultivate crops. Despite this long history of technological innovation, many of us still feel uneasy about things which appear 'unnatural', including an overreliance on our own technological resources rather than God's provision.

Many of the adverse opinions I have heard about Christian engagement online seem to be based on an intuitive suspicion that being present in the digital space diminishes our humanity by weakening our link with Creation and God as our Creator. Moving into a realm where human beings seem to take on a different, 'virtual' nature may feel like a step too far.

Those who are suspicious of technology may draw on the biblical story of the Tower of Babel (Genesis 11.1–9) to demonstrate the dangers of becoming overreliant on human creativity. After the flood, the human beings who remain decide to build a tall tower to reach to the heaven. God comes down to destroy the tower and creates different languages to limit the future communication between different groups of humans as he scatters them throughout the earth. The story of the Tower of Babel is often taken to mean that our technological creativity will lead us into conflict with God. This belief may underlie the historical reluctance of the Church to engage with human technology. But is it right to infer that God disapproves of technology?

In his essay *Holes in the Tower of Babel*,[4] Brent Strawn points out that the builders say they are motivated by the desire to make a name for themselves and to avoid being scattered, and that their unwillingness to be scattered is counter to God's intention for humanity to 'fill the earth and steward it' (Strawn's paraphrase of Genesis 1.26), an intention which is repeated in his command to Noah after the flood: 'And you, be fruitful and multiply, abound on the earth and multiply in it' (Genesis 9.7). Strawn concludes:

> God's punishment, while definitely a reversal of human desire, is not negative: it actually enables the humans to comply with God's initial command. Describing the scattering as 'God's judgment', in this light, is overstated: the judgmental act has nothing to do with the tower as such but with the city (a place of settlement) and the scattering abroad. (p. 8)

It seems that human creativity is part of God's plan, but it is to be used to fulfil God's will, not our own. There are occasions elsewhere in the biblical story of God's relationship with humankind when humans are given very precise technological instructions by God: for example, the instruction to Noah in Genesis 6 to construct the ark to an exact plan, and the detailed instructions to Aaron in Exodus 28 about the clothes he should wear to approach the Tabernacle. These examples suggest that Christians should be involved in technology rather than fearfully retreating away from it.

It is very natural when under threat to hide or resist, but we should not assume that new areas of human creativity are beyond God's scope or interest. Change can cause conflict as some people advocate in its favour and others determine to resist it.

3 *It encourages people to be lazy*

A common critique of Christian websites is that they are encouraging 'laziness' because people don't have to go out outside the home to meet with other Christians and get the benefits of church membership. There is an underlying assumption in this critique that practising the Christian faith should take some effort, and that anything that makes it 'easy' is not going to be an effective form of mission.

The idea that being in an online Christian community is 'easy' is quickly dispelled by experience. Participation in any community takes time and effort, and it is no different if that community happens to be online. Active members of an online community might, for example, contribute to discussion boards on most days, lead or attend worship in real time via live streaming or chat room technology several times a week, pray for people and join in book groups or other study groups, as well as corresponding with other members via email or private messages. In addition, some members will have the responsibility for maintaining the community's online presence and for steering and looking after the community.

We are called to make disciples 'of all nations' (Matthew 28.19–20). This includes going online and making the gospel available to the people we meet there, not just in the words we post but in our behaviour and our relationships. When we make disciples, they are not 'virtual' disciples but real ones.

4 It detracts from the real (offline) church

One of the most pressing worries for the church in the West is the numerical decline in membership. This is largely seen as a consequence of the shift from 'Christendom' – when Christianity was politically and culturally dominant – to 'post-modernity' where no one worldview or set of ideals is seen as overarching. Given these worries about the declining influence of Christianity, it might be supposed that new ways of connecting people with the gospel would be welcomed. Yet as numbers decline, new forms of ministry can, instead, attract opposition from Christians who feel more effort should be invested in strengthening the missional effectiveness of the inherited church rather than dissipated into new and untried models. It is assumed that, by enabling people to participate in Christian community via their electronic communication devices, we are discouraging them from participating in Christian activities offline. Experience suggests the opposite – most online Christian communities have found that participants tend to become more, not less, interested in exploring and expressing their faith offline as a result of their involvement online.

People who are 'seeking' spiritually make up a large proportion of those who find Christian websites and communities. One rationale for creating a Christian presence online is that people who readily use the internet to find out about things are very likely to look there if they want to find out about Christianity. Such 'enquirers' can find out the facts about

Christianity from non-interactive sites which present information in the same way that a book or a noticeboard might present it, but there is a difference between finding out the facts about Christianity and learning how to live as a Christian. To understand what it means to live as a Christian, at some point enquirers need to meet other Christians and experience Jesus-centred community. It follows that people who are seeking Christ online will benefit from finding an online Christian community which is gathered round his person and gospel.

Critics may believe that it is at this point that people should be directed to join an offline church rather than continue with online fellowship. In fact, few online Christian communities would discourage members from engaging with other Christian groups, whether online or offline, because forming networks is inherent to the culture of the internet. Online Christian communities can offer a bridge to engagement with offline churches and are happy to do so.

5 'And day by day the Lord added to their number . . .' (Acts 2.47)

New technology on its own will not reverse decline or make the church more attractive to people who have avoided it up till now. It can, however, enable us to form relationships with people who would not think of setting foot in a church building, and to start to understand how we need to change in order to earn the opportunity to present the gospel.

Why, then, do some Christians feel that the existence of online 'churches' and Christian groups is threatening rather than strengthening? The answer may lie in the models we use to understand the world and the Church's place in it. It is arguable that Western industrialized society is underpinned by a competitive model which the Church has adopted. The push for 'church growth' can put ministers in local churches under pressure to increase their membership, and it is tacitly acknowledged that some numerical growth in churches is by transfer rather than conversion – i.e. as one church adds members another loses them. Assessing ministerial effectiveness by membership numbers can lead to an underlying sense that churches are competing for a finite number of members. This sense of competition will produce church growth strategies which are focused on measurables like attendance and membership rather than other, more nebulous signs of the growth of the kingdom, such as a greater engagement by members in collaborative ministry or a new engagement with the community. If churches are, in effect, competing for members, then the development of online churches may be seen as a threat to offline churches.

If we understand church growth to be about the growth of the kingdom rather than our own individual churches, the picture looks different. Rather than competing for members and resources, we become a network of organizations, with each member strengthened by growth in any part of the network.

Networks occur widely in nature and provide a different model of growth and competition to work alongside 'the survival of the fittest'. Networks are made up of nodes which are linked together by connectors. (For example, in a railway system the nodes are the stations and the connectors are the railway lines.) The more nodes the network has and the stronger the nodes are, the stronger the network is, providing the nodes are connected. Our bodies contain networks which work for our wellbeing, with neural networks transmitting messages to the brain and then back to the rest of the body. The body itself is a meta network, with its parts each contributing to the wellbeing of the whole, not competing for resources but working together. As its name suggests, the world wide web – the www in website addresses – is a network of different websites, hosted by different computers and servers, connected by hyperlinks which direct internet traffic to different addresses.

When St Paul spoke of the body of Christ he could have been speaking of networking, a point picked up in a reworking of Paul's image of the body of Christ in 1 Corinthians by Jonny Baker to show the body of Christ as a network:

> Just as a network, though one, has many small worlds, but all its parts interconnect, so it is with Christ. For we were all baptised by one Spirit and given a portal into the wider network of Christ – whether Orthodox, Emerging, Missional, New Monastic, Catholic, Anglican, Post-denominational, Pentecostal, Baptist, Ana-baptist etc. or any blend of the above the Spirit flows through our networks. So the network of Christ is not made up of one small world but of many interconnected small worlds and hubs.[5]

If we see the worldwide Christian community as a network rather than as a large number of separate, competing denominations and groups, the development of online Christian communities should be seen as a strengthening of the whole, not still more competition for a diminishing number of potential members. In the network model, we should welcome growth in other churches and groups because this strengthens the network to which we ourselves belong, and we should support weaker groups because their weakness detracts from the strength of the network from which we also draw strength.

Christian denominations often came into being through conflict and persecution, so it can feel counter-intuitive for churches to see themselves as members of a wider network whose health depends on the health of the whole. We need to see competition between churches as part of our fallenness and aspire to loving kindness and a generous desire to see others grow in order to benefit the whole Church – including new forms of church which are intended to strengthen the whole body.

6 *What about sacraments?*

The missional imperative to preach the gospel and make disciples has been taken by many different groups to mean 'create communities'. The instinct to create community is sound, because the history of Christianity shows that the faith is best transmitted when it is held and passed in relationships, rather than being broadcast as a one-way message to individuals.

The question of online sacraments arises when we call our online Christian communities 'churches' and therefore raise an expectation that they are exactly equivalent to offline churches and should do the same things.

A widely accepted definition of a sacrament is 'an outward and visible sign of an inward and spiritual grace'. Some churches regard only baptism and Communion as sacraments while others add confirmation, marriage, ordination, reconciliation and extreme unction. Some churches, such as the Salvation Army, do not celebrate sacraments at all. The idea of what happens when a sacrament is celebrated varies widely, as does custom and practice about how sacraments are performed.

In practice, discussion about online sacraments is usually focused on Communion. Receiving Communion is an important aspect of faith to many Christians, and there are many differing opinions about who may preside, who may participate and how it should be celebrated.

Communion can be a divisive issue among Christians, so it is unsurprising that there is no agreement between Christians about whether, or how, Communion can be celebrated online. Some groups have seen 'translating' Communion into the digital medium as straightforward and have introduced words and actions which members accept as a valid Communion. Other groups have decided that offering Communion is bound to lead to conflict, either within the group or outside it, and have therefore avoided it.

In his book *SimChurch*, Douglas Estes explores the dilemma of online Communion. He points out that

> the Bible never puts forward any rules governing the physical or spatial requirements for the Lord's Supper (except for the broken bread and imbibed wine, of course). More specifically, the Bible never puts forward any rules that determine what makes Communion 'real'. Its singular concern seems to be the spiritual condition of the partakers. This is true of the early church fathers as well.[6]

While Estes acknowledges that the majority of online churches he knows of avoid celebrating Communion because of the offence it might give, he comes out strongly in favour of celebrating Communion online, seeing it as a matter of obedience to Jesus' command at the Last Supper and a necessary development if online church is to move out of what he calls its 'beta phase'.[7] He describes two possible methods of celebrating Communion online – symbolically, by meditating on Communion, or via what he calls an 'avatar mediated' Communion, where on-screen avatars partake of an on-screen Communion. Estes acknowledges that the lack of physical elements may lead communities into the risk of 'unintentionally trivializing the Lord's Supper'.[8] However, he does not address the difference between physically consuming the bread and wine (elements) and participating in an on-screen facsimile of consumption, nor does he consider the difference that is created by the presider and those taking Communion being in different physical locations and being unable to share the same bread and wine. He therefore avoids the question of whether sharing the same virtual space can bring us together in such a way as to allow us to share any form of Communion in a meaningful manner.

In the classic definition of a sacrament quoted at the start of the section – 'an outward and visible sign of an inward and spiritual grace' – visibility is the only physical property that is stated to be essential. Since the online world is largely perceived through sight, there seems to be nothing contentious about providing a visible sign of inward grace via an online Communion service. However, the physical proximity of the participants to each other is also implied in the Communion service. The bread and wine brought up from the congregation is blessed and broken by the celebrant before being distributed and consumed by the participants. The action of the Communion service is of breaking, uniting and being sent, and is performed by the whole gathered community, not just by the celebrant – we break the bread (Jesus' body), consume it, are united as the body of Christ through this consumption and are then sent out to serve, breaking the body again to take Christ to the world. The question is whether physically sharing the same bread at Communion is essential for forming us into the body of Christ, or whether, because we are meeting as the body of Christ in the digital space rather than physical space, we can devise a different way of expressing breaking, consumption, unity and being sent which has the same resonance as the offline sacrament.

For people who believe physical proximity is essential to the sacramental nature of Communion, online sacraments will remain an impossibility. Others will be happy to 'receive' in a different way in an online service, believing that this still fulfils Jesus' instruction to 'Do this in remembrance of me' (Luke 22.19).

For those who wish to purse the conundrum of creating an online sacrament, the concept of the **skeuomorph** – which has also been described as 'visual metaphor' – may be helpful:

> Skeuomorph is a term used for any derived object, or thing, that has retained design features that no longer serve any purpose. Although they have an unusual name, they are not uncommon, in fact they are everywhere.
>
> Language is full of skeuomorphs, for example; the meaning of the word 'horsepower' derives from a time when the horses were used to pull carriages and carts. Digital technology incorporates design-features that remind us of their physical equivalents, like the animated 'page turn' at the bottom of some documents.[9]

If we recognize that what we are doing in online community is creating a new form of church that incorporates 'design features' that link us to previous forms of church, this can lead us to a different approach to online sacraments. Instead of simply replicating what we are accustomed to doing offline in the digital environment, we need to reconceptualize the ministry of word and sacrament for the context in which we are working. If in the new environment we replicate the look and feel of what we are used to doing offline, we are not necessarily substituting the virtual elements for tangible, physical ones – we may be using skeuomorphs to refer to, and keep continuity with, the origin of Communion, without them serving any practical purpose in the online ritual we are creating.

While taking Communion with people in the same physical space will never be superseded by an online facsimile, as more online Christian communities are created we need an honest exploration of what an online Communion service might mean spiritually, particularly to people for whom online church is their only possibility of sharing fellowship with other Christians.

3

Where do I start?

The old saying that it takes years to become an overnight success applies just as much to developing an online presence as to any other activity. There is no single, sure-fire way to develop an online presence – our methodology will vary according to our own personality, circumstances and gifts. The process of learning how to present ourselves online and make connections with other people takes time and commitment. Acquiring the skills required can feel painstaking and very slow at the start, but once you have made enough connections to form a network you will find your online activity will start to gather pace.

Like any activity, posting online becomes easier with practice. Learning to post in a style that suits your personality can be referred to as 'finding your voice'. It can be daunting to imagine that millions of internet users may have access to your words, even though in practice very few people read most of what is posted online. Radio presenters are advised to imagine they are talking to just one person, and this is equally helpful advice for our online interactions.[1] Wherever you are posting, respond to the person who has prompted you to write, rather than writing as if the whole internet were going to read it.

Am I called to work online?

Anything we undertake in response to a sense of vocation will draw us from where we feel comfortable towards unfamiliar settings and people. It will also involve spiritual struggles. If you believe you are called to work in an established form of ministry, lay or ordained, your church will have a system to test out that calling and, if it is decided that you have a genuine vocation, will be prepared to invest time and resources into training you to fulfil that role.

Although some churches have set up or resourced online projects, few, if any, have an accredited 'online' or 'digital' ministry in its own right. If you already hold an accredited ministry position in your church and feel called to work online, you may be able to do it as an extension of your existing ministry. If you are not already in a recognized ministry and your church is unable to offer discernment for an online ministry, the only way to find out if your sense of calling is accurate is to test it out by joining an online ministry project or developing your own online presence.

The upside of this lack of recognition for online ministry is that there is a great deal of freedom to develop your ministry imaginatively. The downside is that you may end up working without support from, or accountability to, the wider Church. Everyone in ministry experiences periods of doubt about their effectiveness. If your ministry is not formally recognized, these feelings can be even more difficult to deal with. It is important if you are in this position to establish your own support system, perhaps by finding one or two friends who will pray for you and listen while you talk things through, and/or by seeking out others in online ministry and forming links with them.

Qualities needed for online mission and ministry

There are some qualities which are particularly relevant to working online.

Perseverance

Some projects will attract publicity and members, while others remain unsung. If yours is one of the unsung projects it can sometimes be tempting to assume nobody is interested and give up. A ministry of presence requires that we are reliably there when people want to find us and that we are not put off by setbacks.

Prayerfulness

In common with many Christians, you may not feel you are 'good at prayer'. However, people we meet online may be more willing to ask for prayer than they are to have a discussion. It is important to meet this need. Some people pray for the person immediately, some may post a prayer request in a Christian group, some may keep a prayer diary. Confidentiality is important and so is privacy, so if you record the prayer request online or anywhere on your computer, or share it with others, do so without any identifying details.

It is also important that you should be supported in prayer by others, online, offline or both.

Discernment

It can be hard to determine between those who genuinely need support and those who are using us to entertain themselves or to perpetrate some kind of deceit. If we dedicate our time and energy to people who don't really need it, we may be depriving others with genuine needs.

Self-control

'Never post in anger' is a good principle for online interaction, and can usefully be expanded to include any emotional state which might lead you to post in haste and repent at leisure. Sometimes you will find other people online irritating or annoying. If you feel angered or upset by what someone has written, it is a good idea to wait some time before responding. Being able to walk away from conflict is a great strength in online interactions. Having to have the last word is a weakness.

This is not to say that you should allow people to vent their bad feelings on you. If it is a recurrent pattern, avoid the person or group responsible. If our aim is to build positive relationships, it is better to avoid people or situations which provoke us into negativity or anger.

Humility

Some people use social networking sites to build up their public profile. If you follow people who are doing this, it can be discouraging to compare the numerous successes they report with your own more mundane daily life. We can have no way of judging how significant our activities are to the kingdom of God, but we can be sure that serving God and reaching out to people in his name are the most important things any of us will do. It is helpful to remember that people who announce their importance to the world don't necessarily feel any more important or significant than you do.

There are people online who will take great pleasure in pointing out your errors, whether lapses in spelling, punctuation and grammar, factual errors or spiritual shortcomings. Try and see it as providing innocent enjoyment for the person who is correcting you and bear it with good grace.

Forgiveness

Everyone makes mistakes. Be generous in forgiving others for their temporary lapses of taste, good humour and tact. It could be you who needs forgiveness next time.

Where should I post?

Forums

When the world wide web first developed, it was a 'broadcast' or one-to-many medium – the provider of information or opinion posted it online and other people read it. This kind of web presence is sometimes known as Web 1.0 – the world wide web as it first appeared in its simplest form, with websites simply as a source of information and no interaction possible.

At this stage, internet users who wanted to talk about a particular topic set up email groups or 'lists'. Each email was sent to every list member, enabling the group to share information and discussion. Email discussion groups were largely superseded by the development of interactive forum software which could be added to websites to enable users to comment on the site content, ask questions and interact with other users. Many Christian and other discussion forums exist and can be a good way to start to learn how to interact online. Most forums have rules which are enforced by moderators. Not all forums are equally well run and it is worth looking around and finding forums where you feel comfortable to participate.

Blogging

The move to forum discussions was part of a greater movement towards interactivity, allowing users to post content as well as read it. This development of greater interactivity and user-generated content became known as Web 2.0, indicating a new wave in web use. Web logs, where people posted their thoughts on topics that interested them, became blogs. Blogs which contained interesting or new material about news stories started to be reported by news media, popularizing the idea of the 'citizen journalist' who wrote in the public interest without any pay – or, indeed, any training in many cases. Blogging is still popular, and it is easy to set up and run a blog with very little technical expertise, using an off-the-peg blogging software such as WordPress. Before you set up your own blog, spend some time reading other blogs to get a feel for blogging. Most bloggers are very pleased to receive constructive comments, and many blogs have regular commenters.

Social networking

At first, users of interactive websites could only post the written word, but as software developed it became possible to upload photographs, videos and music to sites without specialist equipment or expensive software. Web 2.0 allowed aspiring writers, musicians, film makers and artists to share their work online without needing to find a publisher or producer. Sites like Myspace, YouTube and SoundCloud provided accounts for people to post their own work and share it with others.

The development of software to allow multi-media sharing led to the creation of social networking sites such as Facebook where all the content is provided by the site users. Your Facebook account allows you to share information about your own life and to comment on what other people are sharing. Users upload their own photos and videos for friends and family to share. It is also easy to share content from elsewhere on the internet. Site users can 'follow' or 'friend' each other to enable them to see and comment on each other's posts, send private messages and chat in real time without leaving the site and without having to ask people for an email address or phone number in order to contact them directly. Social networking sites therefore allow users to 'meet' people online with whom they have a shared acquaintance or a shared interest and become 'friends' without first knowing them offline. This may sound strange to people who have not experienced it, but can be seen as an extension of older forms of social networking such as sports clubs, associations for ex-students of a particular school or college, and writing to penfriends in other countries to learn about their cultures and lives. To use Facebook you need to set up your own account. Details can be found at <www.facebook.com>. Setting up an account is very straightforward, but it is a good idea to use your account settings to set your preferred level of privacy once you have signed in to your account. The privacy settings control who can see what you post, who can send you messages on Facebook and who can see details such as your email address and your birthday.

Microblogging

Another form of social networking is the 'microblogging' site. The best known of these at the time of writing is Twitter. Posts, or 'tweets', are limited to 140 characters, but pictures, videos and audio files can be attached to a tweet. All the posts made by people you follow appear chronologically on your timeline. You can also see what is being posted about a particular topic by searching for it. The most popular topics at any given time are listed as 'trending topics'. It can take a while to build up a Twitter network as it relies on people deciding to follow you and on you following interesting people. However, it can yield a great deal of information about current affairs, including religion. While you will need to sign up for a Twitter account before you can see what other people are posting, this is very simple – all you need do is provide a working email address and create a user name. It is worth keeping your user name relatively short as it appears on all your tweets, and the longer your name is, the fewer characters you will have left for your post. Once you have an account, you have to follow a handful of accounts before you can start posting. Twitter has a very thorough help section which contains further details of how to join up at <https://support.twitter.com/articles/100990-signing-up-with-twitter>.

Virtual worlds

Many Christians have developed church and religious groups within virtual worlds such as Second Life. A virtual world creates an on-screen environment within which the user can control and move a figure called an avatar. Avatars can interact with each other. Communication is usually in text, with speech bubbles appearing above the head of your avatar. There are 'in world' messaging systems to connect with other users. Users can control the environment by creating buildings and other features for which a rent is paid to the site owner. This does require some technical knowledge, although instructions are easy to find online. Role play is a large feature of participation in virtual worlds, with users being able to choose avatars representing animals and supernatural creatures as well as human beings, and identity play is encouraged. Virtual worlds are fast moving and can be difficult to find your way around so the best way in would be to join a Christian or other group you are interested in and learn from more experienced members about how to build a persona and interact.

The best way to find your niche in the digital world is to explore blogs, forums and social networking sites. Bookmark the ones that interest you and visit them frequently to get a feel for how people communicate there, making your own contribution when you are ready. The volume of writing and information you will see every time you go online may feel overwhelming, but remember that you are not obliged to read every word on every web page you visit. Rather than seeing the internet as a reading task to be completed, see it instead as a river of information which you choose to swim in from time to time.

Identity

It used to be accepted practice to create a pseudonym to use online, and thus to conceal your offline identity, but it has now become much more commonplace to post under your own name. There are still some circumstances in which you may feel it is advisable to use a pseudonym – if, for example, you don't want your work colleagues or clients to be able to identify you online. Even if you conceal your offline identity, it is as well to remember that writing under a pseudonym online is no absolute guarantee of privacy. It is almost impossible not to drop crumbs of information about yourself in what you post. It can be tempting to use the relative anonymity of the internet to sound off about people who have annoyed you, but as the saying nearly goes, 'Be sure your tweets will find you out.'

If you choose to be clearly identifiable online, this will reveal your opinions and life choices to everyone you know, not just those people you know online. It is your responsibility how much you choose to disclose about your own life, but be aware that you don't have permission to disclose information about your family, friends and colleagues. If you do want to write observationally about your life, it may be better to create a pseudonymous blog and write a fictionalized account, making it clear that it is entertainment.

It is considered bad form to 'out' someone's identity online if that person clearly does not wish to share it. The most extreme form of this is known as 'doxxing', when someone's real-life identity is traced from details he or she has released online and details such as address, phone number and credit card numbers are made public. Doxxing can be seen as a form of stalking and is a violation of privacy.

Being a Christian online

As God's chosen ones, holy and beloved, clothe yourselves with compassion, kindness, humility, meekness and patience.
(Colossians 3.12)

If we believe that God loves the world and is using us to com-municate that love, then everything we do needs to be measured by that standard – whether other people know that we are Christians or not.

If you have started to engage with people online because you want to use digital media to spread the gospel, you will of course be eager to introduce Christianity into the conversation. If you are seeking to be evangelistic, the same rules apply online as anywhere else – we need to get to know people and to earn the right to share our beliefs. It's usually fairly clear to others if we are befriending them for an ulterior motive.

One quality which many Christians aspire to online is 'authenticity'. It might be assumed that 'being authentic' online means 'presenting yourself exactly as you appear in real life'. The complication is that most of us interact differently with different groups and people. For example, I would not talk to my bishop in a formal meeting in the same way as I would talk to my friends over coffee, and yet I am not being 'inauthentic' in either context – I am just demonstrating my use of 'social register', taking the circumstances in which I'm speaking into account and adjusting my speech to fit them. Perhaps thinking in terms of 'being transparent' is more helpful, so that we aim to communicate clearly, are open about our motivations and don't mislead people or knowingly create a false impression of ourselves.

The idea that we are representing Christianity, in fact Jesus Christ himself, does create a dilemma about how we interact. If we focus on giving the right impression, we run the risk of being less than open and honest about who we are, and there-fore failing to be authentic and transparent. How can we both be open and honest – authentically ourselves – and also reflect the reality of who we are, when we know that sometimes falls short of the Christian ideal we aspire to?

This can be particularly challenging in the context of social media where many people are using their online presence as part of a PR strategy for themselves or their organizations, and see nothing wrong in creating the best impression possible. There is nothing wrong with wanting to give a good impression, but if it is a falsely good impression we will be found out once people start to look more closely. If we don't like the way we appear, we need to work on the substance, not on our image. In particular, if, as Christians, we want to attract people to Jesus, we need to be focused on him ourselves. We are not online to do PR for Jesus – we are online to meet people in his name.

Of course, as Christians we want to represent ourselves as well as possible, so that we represent Jesus and the Church in the best light possible. But if we edit our lives and our personalities to look better than we really are, does this really reflect well on Jesus? The problem with attempting to represent ourselves online as something other than we are is that the truth does tend to shine through the chinks in the façade we create. Unless what we want to claim for ourselves is borne out by the way we behave, people will see the dissonance between who we say we are and who we really are.

When we say something to friends we convey meaning by expression and tone of voice as well as the words we use. What we say online can be quoted out of context, and it may take many hours to correct the impression that our words have created. The saying that 'A lie will go round the world while truth is pulling its boots on' (attributed to, among others, Winston Churchill, Mark Twain and Charles Spurgeon) is even more true when it is being transmitted digitally. This goes for half-truths and misunderstandings as well. However informal online communications may feel, they are in writing and can be retrieved from the memories of computers they have passed through long after you have deleted the original.

Some people advocate operating separate social media accounts, one for people who know you as a 'public Christian' and another for people you know well where you can 'be yourself'. A well-known Christian author or recording artist might attract hundreds of thousands of social media followers. A local church minister might be followed by church members and other local people on a Facebook account which is associated with her church because of her position and not because of their personal relationship. It would raise problems of confidentiality if the person with a 'public' following shared personal conversations with her friends while observed by people who know her only as a public figure. The need for a separate account in this case would become obvious quite quickly.

Operating more than one social media account does require awareness of boundaries and self-discipline. Stating on your personal account that you are expressing 'personal views only' is usually disregarded; if your personal views are at odds with the views your official role would suggest, people will notice this, whichever account you use to express them. Anything that you publish online is in the public domain and can be quoted by journalists, who increasingly use quotes from blogs and social media to enliven their stories. Employers can discipline you for what you post on social media if it relates to work, regardless of whether you have used a pseudonym, or even if you have your account set to maximum privacy.

Support and accountability

Ministry brings pressures, difficulties and dilemmas. It is wise to have support in place before you need it, especially if you are engaged in work that isolates you or that is not understood by others. A spiritual director or accompanier can help you to understand the spiritual dimensions of what you are doing and how to deal with the spiritual challenges you meet. Some potential spiritual directors may say that they do not feel sufficiently knowledgeable, or enthusiastic, about online and digital ministry to offer direction. It is better in this case to continue looking for someone who feels able to help you. It can also be helpful to find someone to offer supervision – i.e. someone who is willing to allow you to debrief your work and talk through any aspects of it which you need to think through. You may also be able to gain peer support from others involved in your own project, or from other people who are developing an online Christian presence.

Cyber space used to be seen as non-territorial and therefore not subject to any particular legal jurisdiction, but as case law develops this is no longer the case. We are all accountable to the laws of our country for what we do online. Be aware of the correct financial structures and other legal requirements such as data protection. If you receive any form of income for your online work you should have clear lines of accountability to those who are paying you, as well as transparent book-keeping. If your income includes grants and donations, it is wise to have a body of trustees to help you remain transparent about finances, even if you do not yet reach the required level of income to register as a charity or a company.

People who are posting under pseudonyms may feel free to say whatever they like, but if you own the site or blog they are posting on you could be liable for any breach of the law. This includes copyright law as well as the law of libel. You are also responsible for maintaining a space where people are safe to post without being subject to abuse or unfair criticism.

Any calling or ministry involves responsibilities. If these responsibilities sound too weighty, it may indicate that you are better contributing to other people's sites or joining an existing ministry rather than setting up your own. As your experience develops, you may find you are more willing to take on the responsibility of setting up your own project.

Measuring reach and influence

Whatever your chosen platform, you will find there are various ways of measuring your reach or influence – sometimes known as metrics. If your aim is to reach people, then obviously it makes sense to measure how many people are being reached. However, measuring online influence is far from straight-forward, and companies who claim to measure influence tend to keep their methodology secret to prevent people 'gaming' their results, i.e. adjusting their actions in order to affect their score.

Most third-party applications which claim to measure your 'reach' or 'influence' say they use algorhythms which are mainly based on click rates – e.g. how many times people click on a particular page or blog post, how many people retweet or 'favourite' your tweets, how many people reply to your posts on Facebook or make you their friend or follow your page. In effect, they are trying to measure how appealing or controversial you are. Well-known people or organizations have a head start in influence measurements since their website, blog and social media accounts will attract more visits, more followers and more replies and retweets than those of private individuals. If you believe that a high influence score will make you appear important – and therefore make your ministry more visible – it can be tempting to try and game the system by posting things which will attract attention. Controversial views cause arguments and this will increase the click rate as people will visit a site again and again to see how the argument is progressing – rather as fights in the street will attract a crowd.

'Influence' sounds like an important thing to measure, but in terms of our online influence it can only measure whether what we post is reposted by others – again, by clicking on a web page. This is a specialized use of 'influence' which does nothing to gauge whether we are communicating effectively with other people. Nobody can measure the effect that your online presence has on people. God's economy is an extravagant one, and a post seen by just one person that helps him or her has had a huge significance in kingdom terms. It will not, however, propel you to the top of any journalist's list of '100 people to follow on Twitter'. A simple measurement of how many people have clicked on your blog or web page, or how many people have followed you on a social networking site, is not, in itself, a measure of how much you have influenced a given individual, or how many individuals you have influenced.

If we are online in order to engage in personal relationships and meaningful dialogue, it is arguable that interacting with thousands of people who follow us simply because we are well known (or notorious) detracts from, rather than adds to, the effectiveness of our interactions. It is tempting to leave online interaction to a few well-resourced and well-known people, but the effect of many Christians interacting through relationships formed in their own circles and networks is greater than a few 'mega-Christians' using social media to broadcast a Christian message outside the context of relationship. While Jesus did preach to large crowds of people, his teaching and healing ministry also took place in small groups, such as the disciples or the group of people he met at Simon's house, or in one-to-one encounters like the woman at the well, the centurion's daughter or the woman with the issue of blood.

In her book *Everyday God*, Paula Gooder writes about the liturgical season known as 'Ordinary Time' and looks at the value of ordinariness in the kingdom of God. She says:

> we also need to recognise that part of the essence of the Kingdom of God is to be 'unsung'. The problem with our celebrity culture, which is as vibrant within the church as outside of it, is that it so often forgets that our calling as Christians is to be servants of all. This does not mean that we are called to be well-known, well-respected, often-thanked servants of all, but that we take on the role of a servant in all its aspects. One of these aspects is to go unnoticed.[2]

Because the digital world moves so fast, one of the most striking statements we can make about the gospel and God's love is to be there for people and to remain there, praying, welcoming, teaching, comforting, and being the good news for whoever needs us.

To be 'incarnational' we need to meet people where they are, not simply broadcast a message to let them know where they can come to meet us. For some people, 'where they are' is online.

4

Pastoral care and relationships

———•·•———

*Which one of you, having a hundred sheep and losing one
of them, does not leave the ninety-nine in the wilderness
and go after the one that is lost until he finds it? When
he has found it, he lays it on his shoulders and rejoices.
And when he comes home, he calls together his friends and
neighbours, saying to them, 'Rejoice with me, for I have found
my sheep that was lost.'*

(Luke 15.4–6)

What sort of pastoral care can be offered online?

'Pastoral care' in a Christian context means supporting and
caring for people who are undergoing problems and crises such
as illness, unemployment, loneliness or bereavement through
practical help, listening and friendship. The word 'pastoral'
relates to Jesus' description of himself as a shepherd, and this
image is a powerful influence on how we perceive pastoral care
in churches, with the minister often standing in for Jesus as the
rescuer and saviour of those in difficulty.

People can be very open about problems online, sharing
news of illnesses and other difficulties widely through social
networking. There is never a shortage of people who might
need support or prayer, and some people will actively seek out
prayer from Christians they know online even if they are not
Christians themselves.

This chapter gives an outline of how pastoral care might
be offered by individuals and how an online community might
offer pastoral care. It also describes some of the difficulties

41

that might arise and suggests ways to avoid these or to manage them.

Helping people in Jesus' name is an enormous privilege. Like everything that is worth doing, it requires some thought and groundwork to get it right, not least because people who come to us expecting help and support will judge the Church as a whole by our response.

Pressures of digital communication for pastoral care

Digital communication offers the opportunity both for conversations in real time (via texting, emailing, instant messaging, Skyping, etc.), where two or more participants talk to each other with no time lags, and for **asynchronous** conversations where different participants contribute at different times, such as an email exchange or a conversation on a forum. This combination can create the impression that pastoral care can be available 'on demand' online, round the clock and seven days a week. It is important to realize at the outset that the limits of online pastoral care are, like the limits of offline pastoral care, determined by the human resources available and not by the method by which they are delivered.

Because messages arrive instantly, this can pressure us into believing we should respond instantly. Unless it appears vital to respond immediately, it is a good discipline to wait before replying, to slow down the rate at which the conversation is flowing. This allows everyone time to reflect. There is a limit to how many pastoral conversations each person can conduct in a day, regardless of whether these are face to face or digital. It is arguable that pastoral relationships which are conducted partially or mainly online are potentially even more intense and demanding than relationships which are largely face to face.

The example of Jesus laying down his life for his flock (John 10.11–16) can create a pressure on pastoral carers to do the same, leading to overcommitment, emotional and spiritual exhaustion and burnout. Pastoral carers, and those responsible for their wellbeing, need to understand that there is a limit to how much time and energy can be spent in online relationships. Intentional boundary setting is therefore vital, both at the start of the project and as it continues. This is an issue that is also increasingly likely to affect ministers whose primary focus is offline as they become more available to their church members online through emails and social networking and the distinction between 'online' and 'offline' relationships becomes less and less clear. For example, clergy who have Facebook accounts have found that these are used by parishioners and others to contact them with urgent requests for attention on days off and even during holidays. If you are in public ministry, as in any other role where you are dealing with people who may encroach on your private life, it is wise to create online spaces which are not accessible to work contacts, such as keeping your personal Facebook account for friends and family and using a church account for communicating with parishioners. It is also important to remember that you are under no obligation to respond to emails and other electronic communications on your day off, any more than you should respond to phone calls about work.

If you find it hard to maintain boundaries between your ministry and your private life, this will spill over into your online relationships and may be an area you could fruitfully discuss with a work supervisor or spiritual director.

Digital ministry can reach you wherever you are if you have a computer, tablet or mobile device with you. There is no 'front door' to put in between yourself and the person in need. Email, social media and instant messaging may enable someone to gain much more immediate access to pastoral supporters than is possible in an offline context. Just as people expect their broadband connection to be 'always on', they may expect the same of an online pastor. Those who minister online may lack the rhythms of engagement and 'down time' that an offline working day gives through travelling to meetings, leaving work to have lunch and so on. Online ministers do not have an unlimited capacity to take on more and more interpersonal work to generate higher contact numbers, and spending too much time relating to others in 'pastoral mode' online can very quickly lead to burnout.

The responsibility for avoiding overload does, of course, rest partly with the ministers themselves, who are responsible for creating and maintaining effective boundaries to give themselves adequate personal time and space. However, this is a shared responsibility with those to whom the minister is accountable; those in a supervisory or permission-giving role need to recognize that projecting their high expectations about numerical engagement or speed of growth on to the leaders of a project may create a pressure which results in ministerial burnout.

The numbers game

John Wesley's statement, 'I look on all the world as my parish'[1] has often been cited as a paradigm for online ministry. Because large social networking sites like Facebook number their users in millions, it is easy to overestimate the number of people that each online project can reach and influence. This creates an expectation that we can reach large numbers of people by using digital media to broadcast or amplify our message, thus allowing a small number of people to reach many more seekers than they might do by other means.

Because online contacts are easy to count, it is tempting to use these as a measure of effectiveness and to assume that the more people are in contact with a project the better, with more contacts meaning more success. The opposite is more likely to be true – although it feels counter-intuitive, a project which attracts large numbers in the short term may stretch its resources far too thinly and fail to live up to user expectations, providing an unappealing experience of Christianity, something which is ultimately counter-productive.

Many people can be reached for Christ online, but there need to be many projects, each devised to suit a particular part of the online landscape, to reach large numbers of people. Each project needs to be seen as part of the wider missional context, with encouragement and support given to others to set up their own.

Numbers are a good measure of how many people we are reaching, but they should not in themselves became the aim of our ministry. We read in Acts that 'every day they added to their number', but we are not told that any particular church growth methodology was in place! The early Christians simply held Christ at the centre of their relationships with each other and this made them an attractive community. Each group of Christians who seek to make Christ known in the world, wherever and however they gather, needs to do likewise.

Developing a personal ministry

If you feel called to mission and ministry online, you may already have become aware of the potential for helping those in pastoral need through seeing people sharing problems and difficulties through social networking. Offering ad hoc pastoral support as and when the need arises is the simplest way to start, but if people begin to seek you out for support this has the potential to become unsustainable in the long term. Operating a one-person online ministry is like setting up a one-person drop-in centre, with no back-up when people become too demanding or when their problems fall outside your ability to help. Dealing with troubled people is emotionally draining, and anyone who is providing such support regularly needs good support and supervision or will soon become exhausted. As you start exploring blogging and social networking, look out for people and groups running online Christian projects, from informal ministries to church-based initiatives. These can be valuable sources of support in developing your own online presence, providing the same sort of informal peer support networks that arise offline between Christians who live and worship in the same area.

If you have no prior experience or training in pastoral care or a similar field, it is unwise to operate as a lone pastoral carer. People with deep-seated difficulties sometimes seek out Christians online because they associate Christianity with unconditional support and help. Training and experience can equip you to manage such expectations, and also to deal with ethical issues, such as confidentiality, which arise when people are sharing their problems with you. If you feel called to support people pastorally online it is advisable to seek out an online Christian group to join whose ministry you can support, or to gain some relevant experience offline. Pastoral gifts are very much more useful when they are used within a supportive framework. It is also important to be able to differentiate between pastoral support, which is offered when people ask for it, and therapeutic intervention, which should only be undertaken by trained professionals operating under ethical guidelines and with appropriate supervision. This is unlikely to be the level of help people expect, or need, from a Christian group.

If your online ministry has developed out of an offline ministry as a church leader or minister, it is important to consider the online pastoral work you undertake as part of your total pastoral load. Also consider whether people who are unable to access you online are disadvantaged if you develop a substantial online ministry, and whether this pastoral load should be shared collaboratively, as it is in many offline churches.

Pastoral care in the online community

Bear one another's burdens, and in this way you will fulfil the law of Christ.

(Galatians 6.2)

The vision of reaching out to people in spiritual or pastoral need is frequently intrinsic to the founding vision of online Christian projects. Many people are willing to talk to Christians and happy to ask for prayer, but don't find it easy to approach a church. This may include people in need of pastoral attention, either because of a crisis or an ongoing problem in their life or because they have started to become aware of a spiritual dimension to life which they are seeking to explore.

In the Gospel of John, Jesus as the shepherd is described as the person who safeguards the whole flock, guarding it from predators. In this image of the shepherd, pastoral care can be seen to be a responsibility of not only caring for individual members in need but also developing the community and creating a safe space in which it can flourish. Thus pastoral care of the individual takes place in the community, and the health of the community is important to the wellbeing of the individual. The online Christian community, like any Christian community, will therefore have to hold the demand from individuals for pastoral care in balance with (or sometimes in tension with) nurturing and growing the whole community through teaching the faith, developing discipleship and encouraging members to discern and carry out its mission and ministry.

Online communities can contribute significantly to someone's pastoral wellbeing when other support is lacking. Access to online Christian communities can compensate for a lack of proximity to 'real-life' Christian fellowship, and online groups can allow people the opportunity to serve rather than being 'clients' who require attention in order to participate at all. Forming online communities is therefore an important way in which Christians can offer pastoral care to people who might look for it there.

Most online communities start with members who have been invited to form the new group. If this initial group becomes close-knit, it can be difficult for new members to find their way into it and it may become a closed group without intending to be. For new members to gain a sense of belonging which roots them into the community for the longer term, they need to find a way into the network of relationships that forms the community. This can happen if they form a relationship with just one existing member, who will then connect them to others. It may happen informally or can be organized more formally through running groups or befriending schemes for new members. Some people will prefer informality while others will be more comfortable with a formal link person, so if it is possible to offer a range of opportunities for new members to connect with the community this ensures that as many needs as possible are met.

The Acts of the Apostles paints a vivid picture of an early Christian community where everyone cared for each other.[2] The simplest, and most attractive, form of Christian pastoral care is when members of a community care for one another without the need for a formal organization. People who are attracted to online ministry often favour simple, non-hierarchical, flat organizations, and so this simple form of pastoral care system often develops spontaneously when a Christian group gather online. While such a system may fulfil the needs of the core group of a project for non-hierarchical relationships, there are several potential pitfalls from the point of view of those joining the community in need of support. Many assume that anything they find online called a 'church' or a 'Christian community' will offer the same standard of care that they would find offline, so it is important not to betray that trust.

The most obvious potential drawback is that it is hard to ensure a consistent quality of care if nobody holds overall responsibility for pastoral care and relationships within the community. While the community described in Acts knew one another well and lived in close proximity, it is possible to join an online community and give away very little about your history and motivations. If there is nobody in overall charge, a member who feels badly dealt with may think there is no way of registering this and simply leave. It is the responsibility of the organizers to ensure that what is offered is carried out with the same level of supervision and accountability as would be in place for offline ministry. People who are not willing to make themselves accountable have no place in ministry, online or offline.

People with difficulties may join an online Christian community because they are looking for help and pastoral attention rather than any other aspect of Christian discipleship. These members may expect, and even demand, the dedicated one-to-one level of pastoral care and interaction that people associate with the traditional image of the vicar. Project leaders may start off by meeting these expectations and offering a very high level of engagement. This is possible at the start of a project when enthusiasm and energy are high, and membership numbers are comparatively low, but it is unsustainable if the community grows numerically. Online communication is usually in writing and so takes longer and requires more care because of the possibility of misunderstandings. One person with complex pastoral needs may therefore take up many more hours online than the same person would do offline.

If limits are not placed on pastoral care in the online community, an ever-escalating demand can be created. This has potentially damaging consequences for all concerned. The mathematics of engagement are the same in any setting where there are 'clients' and 'providers' – the amount of attention available to each member is, roughly speaking, the 'person hours'[3] available divided by the number of people needing attention. Therefore, as membership increases and the scope of the ministry enlarges, it may be necessary to renegotiate the amount of time and pastoral attention that each individual can expect, which will disappoint those people who have become accustomed to a high level of interaction and may result in negative publicity via word of mouth. 'Word of mouth' can include comments on social media and by bloggers, and these may come up on search engines when people are looking for your project for many months after they have been made and amplify the original reach of the criticism. It is very hard to manage the reputation of your project once negative comments are made online. It is better to manage unrealistic expectations from the start of the project. This will not only benefit the team but, in the long run, will also benefit the project by avoiding the generation of negative publicity.

Ministerial burnout is not the only damage that can arise if unsustainable levels of engagement are provided. If the person in need becomes accustomed to a high level of support more or less on demand, he or she can become dependent on the support and grow distressed if it is not available, thus rendering that individual worse off rather than improving his or her situation. If the community becomes focused on meeting a very high level of pastoral need, this can skew its development, attracting more 'clients' and putting off people with different interests from joining. If the client–provider dynamic takes over, the community will stratify into a leadership who are acting as the focal point for a group of dependants rather than a mutually supportive Christian community. Such a community may be filling the immediate needs of the group of people who are receiving pastoral care but it will not be able to engage in any other form of mission.

It takes intentional self-discipline to set and adhere to reasonable boundaries from the start, when there is pressure to do more, but it is not helpful in the long run to start off with a high level of engagement which has to be reduced later on or which affects the viability of the project.

Issues which present in online groups

The golden rule for dealing with people online is 'People will always surprise you.' Some people treat the digital space as a playground or a laboratory for trying out new things; others just find that the lack of physical cues and the apparent anonymity of being online allow aspects of their personality to surface which are usually kept under control. Many of the issues in online communities are no different from those in offline groups, but the way some things develop is different online simply because of the different way communication works.

Grievances

Online Christian communities often attract people who have been unable to settle in offline churches. They may be eager to tell their story; one of the huge strengths of online communities is that they can provide a space for people to say what they need to say and feel listened to. It is easy to become indignant when you hear about how badly another church has treated someone. This reaction may be justified, but remember that this is a subjective account and you are only hearing one side of it, while not forgetting that it is sadly true that churches do cause hurt to members.

People may post about their previous experiences as a form of catharsis or revenge. Clearly, in the interests of fairness, any adverse criticism of other named churches or communities (whether offline or online) should be discouraged. It may be possible to help someone seek reconciliation in private, if that person gives you permission to do so.

Criminal activities and safeguarding

If someone reveals to you that he or she has been a victim of crime in the past, you should encourage that person to raise this in the appropriate place, and tell him or her that you may also have a responsibility to report what you have been told. If anyone discloses any form of abuse, whether current or historic, expert help is required as well as pastoral support. You should ask someone with specialist knowledge, such as the safeguarding officer in your church or social services, for advice on what to do next. It is wise to have a safeguarding policy in place that can be followed should the issue arise, as well as ensuring that your online environment is as safe as possible for everyone. The Child Exploitation and Online Protection Centre (CEOP), at <https://www.ceop.police.uk/safety-centre/>, offers advice and contact details for reporting a crime or suspected crime against a child online.

Disappearing members

Sometimes, people who have been active in the community stop logging in, without any explanation. There is no obvious online equivalent to knocking on someone's door or making a quick phone call to ask how she is, or even asking her friends if she is all right. Reasons for absence might range from illness or bereavement to computer problems or loss of interest. The site administrators will have an email address for everyone who has registered, but emails should be used sparingly. If someone has decided not to participate any more, receiving emails asking 'Where are you?' may not be welcome. Many people dislike receiving unsolicited emails from websites they have joined, and can be worried about how much other information you hold on them. Of course, if you know the person well and have already been given contact details, then an approach is appropriate if he or she is unexpectedly absent. Otherwise, unfortunately there is little you can do to express pastoral concern unless that person chooses to contact you.

Accountability

In Acts chapter 6 we are told that seven deacons were appointed to devote themselves to distributing food to widows so that the leadership could devote themselves to prayer and ministry of the word (Acts 6.1–7). This shows us the development of a pattern of delegated pastoral responsibility within what we might now term 'every-member ministry'. Online churches often follow the same pattern of a very informally structured pastoral care system at the start which needs to become more formalized as numbers, and pastoral demands, grow. This will be easier to achieve when there is already some form of accountability to an outside body such as charity trustees or church oversight structures. In a group which has no external accountability, arguments may arise at this stage about who has the authority to devise or impose an accountability structure in a group which has previously not had any formal hierarchy. The bald fact is that in online communities the person, or people, controlling the administrative functions of your online presence will hold the ultimate power. Anyone who is able to grant or deny access to the online spaces where the project meets, who can ban people from participating and who can decide what is written on the website and whether it stays online, has considerable power over everyone else in the project. This is an uncomfortable power dynamic which is often not overtly stated in online Christian groups where the notional structures are non-hierarchical, but which may suddenly become apparent when decisions about the structure or the future of the group are made.

A situation where everyone has equal status in pastoral ministry may attract people who want to use your community as a base to set up freelance (i.e. unaccountable) ministries, such as healing, on the basis of their own interests or perceived gifts. They may then use the fact that they are based in your community as a form of authentication to others to extend their ministry to other groups or even into the offline church. It is very important not to give recognition to any ministry just because someone claims to be entitled to practise it. No offline minister would dream of turning up in a strange church and immediately asking for ministerial status, and this should not happen online either. Nobody, offline or online, should be practising counselling, spiritual direction or any other form of ministry which may give him or her influence over potentially vulnerable people, without training and supervision. If someone is using your community to demonstrate his or her credibility as a practitioner, it is your responsibility to make sure that that person's training and supervision are adequate.

All counsellors and spiritual directors should be receiving adequate supervision, and if they are working online their supervisor needs to understand that context. If someone is unable to explain what supervision he is receiving he should not be undertaking that form of ministry within your project until he can tell you what arrangements he has made.

Some people may become involved with online ministry because they have been disappointed when trying to pursue a calling to serve the Church offline. People in this situation often have a great deal to offer but need to be carefully supported and deployed, as confidence is often dinted when a sense of calling is not recognized by the Church. It must also be made clear that the same requirements for training and experience apply online as they do offline – you do not want your community used as a 'ministry sandbox' for people to try out ministry on those who may be vulnerable.

5

Online discipleship and spirituality

—————•◦•—————

*Now the eleven disciples went to Galilee, to the mountain
to which Jesus had directed them. When they saw him,
they worshipped him; but some doubted. And Jesus came
and said to them, 'All authority in heaven and on earth
has been given to me. Go therefore and make disciples of
all nations, baptizing them in the name of the Father and
of the Son and of the Holy Spirit, and teaching them to obey
everything that I have commanded you. And remember, I
am with you always, to the end of the age.'*

(Matthew 28.16–20)

Online disciple: a personal story

Jesus said that where two or three are gathered in his name,
he will be present. Many of us have found that this promise
holds good online. Perhaps the very lack of physical presence,
and the time it takes to respond to each other in writing, creates
space in which the Holy Spirit can breathe into our conversations, as well as enabling us to 'listen' to another person more
acutely. This may be the reason that online relationships can
sometimes develop more quickly and become more intense
than offline relationships. My own experience of online discipleship suggests that, for some of us, the digital space can be a
'thin place' where we feel the presence of God more strongly
than in our everyday surroundings.

I was not brought up in a churchgoing household. Although
I had been exposed to Christianity at school, with daily Christian

assemblies and exclusively Christian RE lessons, none of this exposure made me into a Christian; I passed through stages of doubt and outright atheism when I was still at primary school, before becoming interested in New Age teaching and practices[1] such as astrology, palmistry and transcendental meditation through my teens and twenties. In my early thirties, as the mother of two small children, I finally became a Christian after suffering from postnatal depression.

Having become a Christian, I started attending my local parish church and asked to be confirmed. As a preparation, the vicar had several discussions with me where he encouraged me to ask all the questions I could think of, drawing from his wide knowledge of theology to answer them as best he could. This only scratched the surface of what I wanted to know about my new faith, but I soon found that, now I was confirmed, I was regarded as a fully fledged member of the Church. It seemed as if I had somehow qualified as a Christian without knowing I was taking the exams, and was now meant to know everything I needed to know without any further instruction.

Before I became a Christian, I associated Christianity with prohibition. The most memorable phrase in the Ten Commandments for those outside the Church is often 'Thou shalt not . . .' Once I was a Christian, I found out there were 'thou shalts', as well, that caused many Christians a lot of anxiety. I found out that I should be praying and reading the Bible daily and should start 'witnessing' to my friends and neighbours so that they would want to start coming to church. I felt badly equipped to explain my faith or even tell anyone else about it, but I was scared to ask questions at church because that would give away how little I knew. Not uncommonly for a keen new church member, I had already been given leadership and teaching roles very early on in my discipleship journey.

I first went online in the 1990s, when internet access in the home was still a new idea. I had only been a Christian for a few years when I discovered the internet, and so investigating the many Christian websites and discussion boards I found online enabled me to explore the Christian faith through conversation with people from a wide range of faith backgrounds as well as agnostics, sceptics, atheists and people exploring New Age beliefs and practices.

Discussing my faith online allowed me to ask those simple questions that I couldn't ask at church and gradually fill some of the gaps that confirmation preparation had left. It also developed my ability to talk about my faith to other people. My experience of online Christian community was therefore an intrinsic part of my own formation as a Christian and, later, as a minister. It was this experience of encountering so many different points of view, and engaging directly with people who held them, which convinced me that Christians should be online, not just explaining their faith but exploring it in the company of others.

Most importantly, it taught me how many ways of being a Christian there are 'out there'. I encountered people whose view of the Christian faith was very much more conservative than my own, through to people whose Christianity took them way beyond what I understood to be mainstream Christian belief. I also discovered that when you profess your faith online you are open to anyone who wants to attack the idea of Christianity or of faith generally.

Dealing with criticism and attack

Iron sharpens iron, and one person sharpens the wits of another.

(Proverbs 27.17)

If you declare yourself as a Christian on social networking sites by your choice of name or by including your faith in your profile, you will, on occasion, be challenged and even verbally attacked for your views – or for what people assume your views to be.

These encounters can be very difficult and painful but they offer us an opportunity that we are unlikely to get in church to address our critics directly. In that sense, they could be seen to be at the heart of online mission. We may not get the opportunity to explain our faith in words, but we can demonstrate it in our responses to people who attack us.

People who attack Christians online usually do so for a reason. These reasons vary, so it is a good idea to work out what is motivating someone to attack you rather than dismiss the person out of hand. Sometimes people simply enjoy starting fights and upsetting people online, and find Christians are easy to goad into an argument. Others have a dislike of organized religion in general or of Christianity in particular, and will throw some well-worn arguments or criticisms your way without being at all interested in your answer. Some will have had damaging experiences at the hands of other Christians which have left them angry and possibly scarred, and they want someone to hear and acknowledge what they have experienced.

It depends on your temperament and your reasons for being online how you respond to these challenges. Some people thrive on debate and can participate in lively discussions without feeling emotionally affected. I don't enjoy arguing and can easily become emotionally involved, so I am usually completely open about the fact that I don't enjoy arguments for their own sake and withdraw. It's important to know what your strengths are, and I know that I am much better at dialogue than debate. People who excel at factual, point-by-point debate may find it more difficult to participate in the sort of dialogues I enjoy, where there are no clear winners or losers but an increase in mutual understanding.

If people are aggressive, it's important to try and work out what is behind the aggression. If someone has a general antagonism to Christianity, or is looking for a fight, there is little point trying to placate him or her – this person is not looking for a discussion but for someone to use as a verbal punchbag.

We are under no obligation as Christians to offer ourselves to be the target of other people's enmity. Sometimes people are aggressive because they, or those close to them, have been hurt by the Church or by Christians. In this case, listening and responding empathetically is helpful; arguing that they are wrong to feel as they do, or defending the actions that caused them distress, is more likely to reinforce their distress. As the book of Proverbs reminds us, 'A soft answer turns away wrath, but a harsh word stirs up anger' (Proverbs 15.1).

Sometimes we need to put our need to defend ourselves or our faith to one side. If our aim is to help people understand God's love for them, that might sometimes mean we need to sit on our hands – metaphorically or physically – and find instead the soft answer that keeps our dialogue open.

Discipleship and dialogue

Followers of Christ never stop being disciples. Being discipled is as important for long-established as for new Christians. It's a task for life.[2]

Mission and ministry are the business of the whole Church, and always have been. Jesus chose disciples to travel with him not just as a support group but in order to teach them so that they could continue his ministry. Christianity was not spread by sending Bibles around the world – indeed, there were not yet any Bibles to send – but by people travelling and sharing their enthusiasm and conviction about the good news of Jesus' life, death and resurrection.

In recent years, the church in the West has moved into what is called a post-Christendom era. Christianity is no longer the default belief system and the number of professing Christians has decreased as a proportion of the population. As the average age of Christians increases, there is a fear that the church will die out completely unless more people are evangelized. One outcome of this is that there is a new enthusiasm for discipleship as the foundation for the mission and ministry of the Church.[3] Discipleship is a process of education and formation which enables Christians to learn about their faith and to become spiritually mature. It is also the basis for collaborative, every-member ministry which reaches out into people's communities and workplaces to places where accredited ministers cannot reach.

One way in which discipleship is being promoted is by courses, such as the Pilgrim Course, which seek to encourage groups of Christians to discuss and explore their faith together. While there is a teaching input into such courses, they are also open-ended, allowing group members to put their own ideas and experiences forward. Such courses can easily be run online, allowing them to be extended to people who are unable to attend in person because of distance or for other reasons.

There are also other, more spontaneous, less organized opportunities for discipleship online as well, both on social networking sites and on Christian discussion forums. Although Twitter is often dismissed as a place where people share trivial details of their lives, I have seen and participated in many searching discussions about faith. Such discussions happen unpredictably, starting out between people who know each other and gathering participants as people 'overhear' what is being discussed and join in because it interests them; they usually last no longer than half an hour. The old 'broadcast' method of teaching the faith – where one person who is authorized by the Church distributes his or her knowledge to many through preaching or writing – is difficult to impose online, where people are used to questioning and responding. The participative and mutual ethos of online communications means people learn from each other in an organic way. When we are participating in social networking sites, we are, like St Paul, preaching 'in the market-place' where people are gathered,[4] rather than asking them to come to our own space to listen to what we want to tell them. This level of participation and lack of authority might sound dangerous, until we remember that the faith was first transmitted by enthusiastic people entering into dialogue with whoever happened to be there, rather than by distributing books or pamphlets. Of course, open discussions can sometimes lead to misunderstandings and misinterpretations – as occasionally happened in the early church. But collaborative learning creates an energy and enthusiasm that can sometimes be missing when we see faith as something that we must learn by listening quietly to the experts.[5] We need 'experts' who are humble enough to learn how to offer their knowledge and theological reflections in the cut and thrust of a spontaneous discussion rather than as a lecture, as they may have done before.

Prayer

Many Christians will have had the experience of a non-believing friend asking them to pray. People seem to believe in prayer, as a simple act of asking 'someone up there' for help, even if they find it hard to believe in God. A search on Twitter for the words 'pray' and 'prayer' demonstrates that, whatever the state of the Church, prayer is still very popular. People from the Pope downwards post their prayers on Twitter, perhaps in the hope that someone will see and join in with their prayer, but perhaps also with the a feeling that the act of typing the prayer online is, in itself, praying – as if they believe at some level that God, or whoever might answer prayers, is present online or at least aware of what people are doing there.

I have seen prayers for people taking exams, people who are facing their own illness or death or those of a loved one, people seeking God's will in their lives, people who simply need to feel God's presence – whatever it is, if people who would not go into a church to post a prayer request will post prayers online, it suggests that they believe God is listening to them there.

Twitter's 'trending topics' show the subjects that the greatest number of people are talking about at any given point in the day, often preceded with a hashtag (#). It is not surprising that #Easter and #Christmas are always trending topics at the appropriate time of year. It's possibly a little more surprising that prayers for difficult and sad situations in the news often become trending topics. For example, in March 2012 the Bolton Wanderers footballer Fabrice Muamba collapsed on the pitch with a cardiac arrest during a match with Tottenham Hotspur, and it took 78 minutes for his heart to be restarted. His family asked for prayers for him, and #PrayforMuamba trended almost immediately and continued until the news came that he was expected to recover.

Commenting on this phenomenon, BBC journalist Mark Easton wrote:

> Have you prayed for Fabrice Muamba today? His family are exhorting the country to believe in the power of prayer, and I suspect many millions of Britons, whether they have faith or not, will have felt moved to offer a silent appeal to an invisible power asking that the young footballer pull through.
>
> The front page of today's *Sun* newspaper is devoted to the headline 'God is in control' below the subheading 'Praying for Muamba'. 'In God's hands,' says the *Daily Star*. Chelsea defender Gary Cahill pulled off his shirt after scoring yesterday to reveal a vest encouraging supporters to 'Pray 4 Muamba', his former team-mate.[6]

Easton goes on to comment on the popularity of prayer in an increasingly secular society, adding

> A study in Britain of 4,000 12–15-year-olds conducted in 1992 by the academic and Anglican priest Leslie Francis found that 'as many as one young person in every three who never has contact with church nonetheless prays at least occasionally'. The frequency of personal prayer, he concluded, is 'an important predictor of perceived purpose in life'.[7]

Praying for people can take us beyond arguments about God's existence or issues of doctrine and right to the heart of Christian belief – God is with us and loves us. As Christians online, we can give the gift of our prayers to anyone who asks for them.

Worship

Online worship happens in a number of formats. When a service is transmitted via the internet this is known as **live streaming**. These forms of worship differ from broadcasting, in that there is a relational element between those who are at the church service in person and those who are participating via the internet. Some churches have been providing live streaming of christenings and weddings as well as the usual Sunday services since the technology became economically available to use, offering a way of involving friends and relatives who are unable to attend in person.[8] Live streaming of services has been combined with Communion by extension by some parish churches, so that people in a residential home who are unable to get to church may watch a Communion service at their local church via the internet and then receive Communion by extension,[9] brought to them directly from that service. Churches such as LiveChurch TV in the USA show live worship services online to localized gatherings or 'campuses' who meet in real time to join in with the worship.

Many online Christian communities have created forms of worship which happen exclusively online, with people 'meeting' in digital space. The development of virtual worlds such as Second Life enable churches and other 'sacred spaces' to be created online, where avatars can move and speak on screen as directed by the person they represent. Worship in chat rooms can also be remarkably effective, either just using typed words on screen or with the addition of audio and video files to add music and readings. Instant messaging services such as

Google Plus can be used to create temporary rooms for people to join together in prayer and worship at agreed times. Prayers can be shared in words. The addition of emoticons – small pictures or symbols expressing different emotions and actions, such as :-) for a smile, :-(for sadness, ['] for a candle and \0/ for rejoicing – can enable people to communicate feelings without having to put them into words.

Online worship may appear to be the ultimate in convenience, but setting aside time and space to participate requires self-discipline and commitment. The distractions of social networking and email programmes are never far away when you are online and, again, it requires self-discipline to make yourself fully available for prayer and worship. There is a knack to chat room or instant messaging conversations – each person in the group needs to be committed to 'listening' to others and responding, as well as saying what he or she wants to say. Online conversations can enable people to listen very carefully to each other.

The timing of worship will vary depending on the needs of the community. Streamed services will normally take place at times when we traditionally expect church services to happen, and will suit the timetables of the people who are leading them. In an online Christian community meeting in a chat room, because there is no building to unlock and prepare and no worship band to tune up, it may appear feasible to put on a number of worship events a week at different times so that all those who might wish to attend can find a service to suit them. In practice this can be counter-productive, as attendance is spread out over a number of services with poor or no attendance at each one and with no sense of being part of a worshipping community. It is better to start off with one or two services or meetings a week and stick to those times so people start to remember when worship is each week. People may ask for services at specific times, such as Christmas Day, but it is a good idea to find out if they themselves are planning to attend!

There can be a tendency to develop a 'wish list' mentality, where people are asking not for things they want themselves but for things that they think should be available on principle, without thinking that someone will have to make the time available to lead a service even if nobody intends to turn up. At major festivals, it is often helpful to plan events which complement what is going to be available in churches and on television and radio. For example, there will be carol concerts and Christmas Day services available, but the recent innovation of a more contemplative 'Blue Christmas' service for people who are finding Christmas difficult might be a helpful addition which could be offered online. It is good practice to look at what others are offering and encourage participation. For example, if another group is offering a carol service online which is easy to access, why not support it rather than setting up a rival event?

Worship leaders should be people who have been attending for long enough to know how to lead a simple service, and who have no problems working within the doctrinal basis of your group if it has one. If you are working within a particular denomination or church stream, there may be particular requirements about training and accreditation for people leading services online, as there are offline. A baseline might be that someone should be 'in good standing' in the community.

Materials for worship and prayer services might be written within the community, but there are also many resources, online and offline, that can be adapted. Nothing should be published on your website without appropriate permission from the copyright holder – this is usually readily given. In chat room worship, which is mainly word-based, the tendency is to use far too many words; try to think about creating space for reflection between the words. If you are inviting participation, be clear about what is being asked, e.g. 'In this time of prayer, please feel free to type your prayer requests, or simply to post a candle . . .' and be clear about what is happening, e.g. 'We will now say the

Lord's Prayer in our own time. Please type "Amen" when you come to the end.'[10]

Online worship gives great scope for developing community. It is good to have a core of people who worship together, but remember the aim is quality of experience, not quantity of worshippers.

Spiritual direction and accompaniment

Spiritual direction has been described as

> help given from one Christian to another which enables that person to pay attention to God's personal communication to him or her, to respond to this personally communicating God, to grow in intimacy with this God, and to live out the consequences of the relationship.[11]

It takes more than goodwill and an interest in other people to be a spiritual director – it also needs patience, stamina, tact and commitment. It is exciting to see people take strides in their faith journey, but they may become 'stuck' before they are able to move forward. It can take many hours of listening to someone seemingly going round in circles before that person reaches a new insight.[12]

As well as personal qualities and skills, a spiritual director also needs a good understanding of confidentiality – including how to deal with any issues that arise which may have legal implications, such as the disclosure of a crime.

For all these reasons, it is important that anyone offering spiritual direction, whether online or offline, should have adequate training and be in a continuing relationship with a supervisor. Goodwill and the desire to help people in their faith journey are a good start, but we also need the ability and skills to help or we can end up unintentionally doing harm. As the fourth-century anchorite Abba Paphnutius put it: 'I have seen a man on the bank of a river buried up to his knees in mud and some men came to help him out, but they pushed him further in up to his neck.'[13]

There are many organizations in the UK offering short courses in different aspects of spirituality as well as longer training courses for people who wish to become spiritual directors, such as the Retreat Association and the London Spirituality Centre.[14] Another route to explore would be to ask what is offered by your own or another denomination, either locally or in other areas. Any course you attend should be able to advise you about finding a supervisor.

Online spiritual direction may be helpful to people who are unable to travel to meet a director in person, either because there is nobody available locally or because they have constraints such as illness, lack of mobility or family commitments. The same limitations apply to online direction as they do to online relationships generally – the lack of a physical presence emphasizes words and reduces the information available from the body language and tone of voice of the participants. Directors are often recommended to conduct meetings via Skype or another programme which allows the director and the directee to see and hear each other, rather than by typing words into a chat programme. This can provide some of the information that is missing in a conversation which is conducted only by text. It also means that both participants can see that the other person remains focused throughout the meeting and is not tempted to multitask!

Within an online Christian community, there is the opportunity to share each other's faith journeys in a group setting. This requires trust and a shared understanding of confidentiality and ground rules, so is better confined to a closed forum rather than conducted on a public site which anyone can read. A simple format might be to draw up a rota so that each person posts in turn about an issue or situation he or she wishes to consider, then others reflect and comment if they feel they have something useful to say. The convenor of the group can remind people when it is their turn to post and encourage people to contribute constructively. As in any Christian community, people may also support each other informally.

Online retreats

To retreat is to withdraw or fall back. In battle, the retreat is sounded when an army is unable to gain a victory. The retreat enables resources to be preserved and a new plan to be formulated.

In our spiritual lives, there are also times when we need to withdraw from whatever struggles we are engaged in and renew ourselves by renewing our relationship with God, the source of hope and peace in our lives, so that we return to our everyday lives refreshed and resourced.

Going on retreat is usually associated with a journey to a monastery or a retreat house so that we are physically as well as spiritually separated from our everyday lives. The main point of a retreat is, however, not the physical relocation but the spiritual reorientation it offers. Of course, we can set time aside on our own to pray, but the sense of a shared time of prayer and openness to God can be achieved through sharing aspects of it with others online.

Each retreat group will need to make its own arrangements depending on the technology available to members of the group. Group members will all need to be able to access a chat room, chat programme or another virtual space that can be shared. Recorded readings, reflections, prayers and music can be offered as audio or video via media-sharing sites like YouTube and SoundCloud. Participants can undertake shared physical actions, such as lighting candles, in their own space, and can share times of discussion or open prayer. They should be offered the opportunity to speak to someone or ask for prayer in private if they need it, just as they would be in an offline retreat.

Discipleship is a lifetime's journey for most of us. Online relationships provide opportunities to share this journey with people we may not meet in any other setting, and to learn about our faith from a wide range of people.

The Fresh Expressions leaflet 'God wants people to become disciples of Jesus' says of discipleship:

> It's a rather limited vision to bring more people into the church just so that they can bring more people into the church. (Sometimes the emphasis on evangelism can read like that.) Drawing individuals to Christ should bear kingdom fruit by enhancing their ability – through being discipled – to love other people, promote justice and care for creation.

It suggests a list of principles to promote good discipleship in a Christian community:

- listen to those you are seeking to disciple;
- address the whole of life;
- nurture community;
- provide plenty of support;
- rethink worship, learning and spiritual practices;
- encourage reliance on the Holy Spirit;
- remember that discipleship is changing.

All these principles can be encouraged in online communities and can help more people become kingdom-focused servants of God wherever they find themselves in the world, whether online or offline.

6

Dealing with difficult and disruptive people

-------◆•◆-------

All communities have to deal with difficult behaviour from time to time, and Christian communities, online or offline, are no exception.

Over the last few years, cases of 'cyber bullying' on social networking sites, leading the victims to despair and even suicide, have been extensively reported. In the last few years the UK police have brought successful prosecutions of people who have abused others and threatened them with actual bodily harm through social media sites. In January 2014, Isabella Sorley and John Nimmo appeared at Westminster Magistrates' Court, where they were jailed for 12 and 8 weeks respectively after pleading guilty to sending menacing public messages over the electronic communication network. Sorley and Nimmo used multiple accounts to abuse and threaten feminist campaigner Caroline Criado-Perez and MP Stella Creasy after their involvement in a successful campaign for a female figure to appear on a Bank of England note. Messages included graphic threats of rape and murder. Judge Howard Riddle said it was 'hard to imagine more extreme threats' and that the perpetrators' anonymity increased the fear felt by Ms Criado-Perez and Ms Creasy. Caroline Criado-Perez said the effects on her had been 'life changing' and Ms Creasy had had a panic button installed in her home.[1]

Cases like this may make people wary of coming into contact with aggressive or threatening behaviour if they become involved

with online ministry, but it's important to keep it in proportion – the cases that hit the headlines are extreme examples.
As case law develops, it is becoming clear that being online
does not give impunity from prosecution for offensive or illegal
behaviour. However, most cases of bad behaviour will not
breach any laws and need to be dealt with by the administrators
or owners of the site or page. The day-to-day difficulties
presented by dealing with people online are usually far less
dramatic that the ones that hit the headlines. Most of the
bad behaviour you will deal with online is a nuisance rather
than threatening, but it does need to be dealt with. Most problem behaviour is attention-seeking, and if you allow such
behaviour to escalate you will end up spending a lot of time
on troublemakers rather than fulfilling the original aims of
your project.

Words and phrases we use to refer to the online environment,
like 'virtual' and 'cyber space', may suggest that our online relationships are less intense than the relationships we have with
people who are physically near us, but the opposite is often
true. Online relationships can be very emotionally engaging
because it feels as if the other person is very closely and directly
in touch with us through our computers or mobile phones.[2]
Many genuine friendships, and even romantic relationships,
start online. If conflict arises in the online context, that can also
be experienced very intensely. People can be very much more
outspoken and emotionally volatile online than they are in face-
to-face relationships. Negative or aggressive statements about
us come into our computer or phone, creating a sense that the
aggressor is inside our personal space, or even in our heads.
This can be increased if 'dog piling' – whereby an attack by one
person provokes further attacks on the same individual from
the attacker's supporters – takes place. Once you have been
attacked, the fear of further attacks can make turning on the
computer or looking at your phone very stressful. It is hard
to explain how stressful online conflict can be to anyone who

has not experienced it. It is therefore important to work with a team or to have the support and supervision of someone who can understand the nature of working online.[3]

Trolling and flaming

Unfortunately, the internet is full of people who seek out opportunities to cause conflict and abuse people. Christians who decide to set up online communities may assume that they will be exempt from such problems, but Christian sites are not immune from bad behaviour, especially if your aim is to connect with non-Christians.

The Church of Fools website, set up in 2004, was under attack from trolls and hackers from day one. Part of the attraction of the Church of Fools was that it provided a well-designed 3D virtual world which was free to use – a rarity in 2004. While it gave enough visual cues to Christians to encourage them to behave as if they were in church, to those unfamiliar with church it offered the same potential as a gaming site and that is how they related to it.[4] What looked like bad behaviour in the context of 'church' was often playful if understood as the behaviour of unchurched young people who wanted somewhere to hang out.

One account of the Church of Fools notes:

> apart from a majority of voices in praise and agreement, there arose a multitude of conflicts, both during and apart from the services. For one thing, the church suffered multiple attacks by hackers, rogue programmers who tried to gain control over the software behind the Church of Fools. Hacking forced the operators to step up security measures. Significantly, then, most of the disturbances did not originate outside but rather within the virtual church environment. The main problem was a host of disruptive visitors, so-called trolls, who forced the organisers to remove certain applications such as the 'shout' function of written chat by which people could 'speak' in the church.[5]

The word 'trolling', when used about online behaviour, is related to 'trawling', and in this sense means 'fishing for a response'. Online trolling is behaviour which trolls or fishes for an intense emotional response from others.[6] It is more helpful to think about trolling as a pattern of behaviour that needs to be discouraged rather than labelling specific individuals as 'trolls' who need to be controlled. There are different reasons for disruptive behaviour. Some people, especially those who are inexperienced with online communication, may simply not realize the effect of what they are doing – such as continually asking the same questions – on other people. At the other end of the spectrum there are undoubtedly a few people who enjoy causing arguments and conflict in online groups. People who have been hurt or angered by a church or Christians will sometimes seek out Christians online in order to vent their anger or raise their grievances. A very small minority of atheists object to Christianity so strongly that they will use any opportunity they find online to ridicule Christianity and Christians, including coming on to Christian websites to take issue with the beliefs expressed there. The majority of online attacks seem to come from people who simply enjoy a good argument and will prolong it as far as possible.[7]

It is difficult to see a way out when you are under attack from someone who appears angry, irrational and unpredictable.[8] Trolling behaviour can include 'flaming'. Flaming is posting angrily and aggressively, using extreme language and insults. It is often aimed at an individual or group and may contain libellous material which needs to be removed. It always makes very unpleasant reading and always diverts the discussion away from the topic in hand and towards the behaviour of the person who has been flaming. At worst, flaming exposes underlying conflicts and encourages other people to join in. This can spread very quickly across a website as every discussion is diverted into a discussion of the flamer and his or her target.

The dilemma with disruptive behaviour in a missional context is that self-expression and playfulness for some people can create what feels like an unsafe or undesirable environment for others. If we see online mission as contextual, then if we seek to impose our own concept of suitable behaviour on our visitors we may defeat our aim of connecting with people outside mainstream church culture. However, if we allow free rein to people to express themselves in whatever way they want, we risk damage to anyone vulnerable who may be just as much in need of the gospel as those who are behaving this way. This dilemma can make Christian sites particularly vulnerable to manipulation by a certain type of internet user who enjoys causing conflict and finds it entertaining to see how far a Christian community can be pushed while it tries to be tolerant and accepting.

Dealing with problem behaviour

Dealing with and discouraging problem behaviour can be very time-consuming. Trolling can be particularly hard to deal with in a Christian context because as Christians we rightly feel that we should make an effort to understand people and accommodate them. This makes Christian sites irresistible to a certain kind of troll who is aware that Christians believe they should 'turn the other cheek' and finds it entertaining to see how much bad behaviour will be tolerated in a Christian community before its members get angry and sanctions are applied. The received wisdom among users of online forums is 'Don't feed the troll' – i.e. do not rise to behaviour which is clearly meant to provoke a reaction. This is good advice for individual users of forums or social networks, but very bad advice for people who are running forums, blogs or pages. If such behaviour is not dealt with it will spread to other users and attract new users who are looking for a space where they can flame other people with impunity. There are even online communities where members exchange information about possible sites to troll.

In his book *In Sheep's Clothing*, subtitled *Understanding and dealing with manipulative people*, George Simon describes how certain people can manipulate our desire to help:

> we've been pre-programmed to believe that people only exhibit problem behaviors when they're 'troubled' about something inside or anxious about something. We've also been taught that people only aggress when they're attacked in some way. So, even when our gut tells us that someone is attacking us for no good reason, or merely trying to overpower us, we don't readily accept the notions. We usually start to wonder what's bothering the person so badly 'underneath it all' that's making them act in such a disturbing way. We may try to analyze the situation to death instead of simply responding to the attack. We almost never think that the person is fighting to get what they want, to have their way with us, or to gain the upper hand. And, when we view them as primarily hurting in some way, we strive to understand as opposed to taking care of ourselves.[9]

Simon is writing about what he terms 'covert aggression', which is expressed through manipulative and disruptive behaviour in therapeutic and pastoral settings, including churches. His view is that we should deal with the behaviour, not the assumed causes. This is especially helpful in the online context where we simply cannot know why someone is acting in a particular way and so may delay dealing with the disruptive behaviour in case we make things worse for him or her. Even if people have underlying difficulties that they are acting out by verbally abusing us and disrupting our site, allowing them free rein to disrupt is not going to help them.

Most disruptive behaviour online seems to come from people who enjoy causing problems, whether by infecting people's computers with viruses or disrupting a community. If you run a website, web page or blog which is overtly Christian, you have a responsibility to ensure that users don't mistreat each other.

The responsibility of a community leader is to the community that is being disrupted, not to the newcomer with an apparent need to disrupt.

Setting boundaries – aims and terms and conditions

The attraction of working online is that it puts us into contact with a wide range of people, but this is also a challenge. The ethos of the internet appears to be one of spontaneity and freedom of expression. There is no overall authority structure, so it is up to the administrators of a site, page or blog to create and maintain the right environment for positive engagement and to discourage negative behaviour. Not everyone who visits a website is supportive of its aims, and some will be actively disruptive. If we want to create a welcoming online environment, we have to assert our own values in engaging with other people. In John chapter 10, Jesus uses the image of a shepherd to illustrate the need for boundaries in order to keep the flock safe, and if we are creating a space that is intentionally Christian online we need to follow his example.[10]

The keys to managing difficult behaviour are being clear about your aims, setting boundaries and enforcing them consistently. Before writing any rules, it is important to decide on your aims and the target group or groups for your activity, and to write these down.[11] When people are disruptive it can be helpful to remind yourself of your aims and the people you wish to contact. It will almost always be the case that a disruptive person who is causing the problem is not part of the group you are aiming to serve. For example, you may wish to set up a space where new Christians and non-Christians can ask questions about Christianity, but find that regular churchgoers visit your forums to express anger about what is happening in the local or national church. If you find that you are spending most of your time dealing with disruptive and attention-seeking behaviour from people who fall outside your target group, you need to reassert your priorities. This will usually mean that you decide not to engage with that particular issue, and say so.

Most websites ask users to agree to their terms and conditions (T&Cs) before allowing them to create an account. The T&Cs can include rules and/or behaviour guidelines, as well as more basic legal requirements such as avoiding copyright infringements and libellous statements. These should state who has the authority to make decisions about how the site is used, such as the site administrator. If you are providing an online meeting place, you can draw a line under an argument that is causing bad feeling and ask people to stop. Referring to the T&Cs and reminding users that they signed up to them can curtail arguments about what is and isn't allowable.[12] Anyone who tries to restart an argument after that point can be reminded that joining involved agreeing to accept the site administrator's decisions. If he or she continues after this then a suspension or ban can be used to enforce the rules. It is completely reasonable to use this power if someone continually breaches the T&Cs after being warned that this could result in a ban. However, such powers should be used very sparingly or it becomes counterproductive. It's important to post warnings and explain which rules have been broken before banning someone because, if someone is banned and nobody understands why, it will make other people wary of posting. In practice, it is rare that somebody will push a confrontation with site managers that far, especially if the potential consequences are spelt out clearly at an early stage.

If you are running a blog or a social networking page on a website you don't own, you can still state the terms of engagement. You will still have the power to remove someone from the group or to prevent that person from posting, and you can refuse to accept further contributions from people who are unwilling or unable to keep your rules.

Disruptive people who are told they are breaking the rules will often try to draw you into an argument about the meaning of the rules or your right to enforce them. The 'broken-record technique' – where you continue asserting the point you want to make rather than getting drawn into an argument about it – can be useful to counter this. There is no point in arguing with someone who clearly enjoys arguing for its own sake. It is important to remain courteous and not to descend to bad language or name-calling, even when these have been used against you. It is important that moderators and anyone else with a leadership role should model the behaviour they wish to promote in users. It is pointless demanding courtesy from users if those in authority are discourteous.

Establishing and maintaining firm boundaries is hard work and may give rise to accusations of authoritarianism, particularly from the people whose behaviour is being moderated. You may even be told that you are 'not Christian'. In this situation it is important to remind yourself of your vision statement and/or aims and objectives and the needs you are setting out to meet. Unless your original aim was to provide a place where people could have arguments, then disruptive behaviour is distracting you from your original vision.

It is important to remember that our concern should be for everyone who uses our site or page, not just for those who demand the most attention. Aggressive and disruptive behaviour can make other people feel unsafe and unwilling to participate. It is important to be clear about your own reasons for engaging online and to avoid being side-tracked into providing attention and entertainment for one or two disruptive people. The motive for deliberately disruptive behaviour is often enjoyment. Some people enjoy starting an argument then standing back and watching it, both online and offline.

It is very important to apply the same standards of behaviour to everyone, regardless of what you think lies behind someone's behaviour. If allowances are made for some individuals while others are moderated very firmly, this confuses other members and undermines the standards of behaviour you are trying to set.

Identity play and impersonation

Virtual worlds (such as Second Life) and multi-user game-playing sites encourage people to assume an 'in world' identity. On more run-of-the-mill discussion boards and blogs it is generally frowned on to pretend to be something you're not or to create multiple personas. For those who treat the internet as a playground, identity games can provide a lot of fun. It can give rise to distrust and distress if a member of an online community turns out to be a fake persona created for the entertainment of the person, or people, behind it.

Pseudonyms and pseudonymity

There is a long-standing tradition of using pseudonyms when posting online. There may be a number of reasons why people prefer to use a pseudonym, including being uncomfortable about other people seeing them using a particular site – and this could apply to Christian websites as much as any others. It is important to treat people's privacy seriously.

Social networking sites such as Facebook ask for real-life names to be used. If you are found to be operating a fake identity on Facebook you can be banned. This convention has increased the number of people who post under their own names on blogs and forums, but it is still acceptable to use a pseudonym rather than your real name when joining internet forums or posting on blogs.[13]

People who use pseudonyms to maintain their privacy may conceal other potential identifying details such as their location, and some may maintain the pseudonym to the extent that they write as if they are the persona they have created and do not post any personal details relating to their offline life.[14] Keeping your true identity hidden behind a pseudonym in this way is known as 'pseudonymity'. Pseudonymity at this level is very hard to maintain because it comes naturally to most of us to share details of our lives with others when we are getting to know them.

Some people go further than pseudonymity and create a different identity which they pretend is a real person. Even people who post with their own names may behave more freely and unreasonably than they would if they were meeting people face to face, and hiding behind a fake persona can create an even greater sense of freedom, which can in turn lead to disruptive behaviour.

It is sometimes suggested that Christians should maintain separate social networking accounts for 'real friends' (where, presumably, we can let our hair down) and 'Christian contacts'. This implies that when we befriend people in Jesus' name we are creating a 'Christian' persona which is different from the person we 'really' are. This is not unlike creating a pseudonymous personality online, with the same difficulties – it is difficult, or even impossible, to build a genuine relationship with someone if you are editing what you say to create the right impression rather than being yourself. If you are running an overtly Christian online group or website, it is better to be completely transparent about your offline identity. This creates accountability and reminds us to be consistent about how we present ourselves online and offline.

Sock puppets

The most common identity game is to create two or more personas who are believed to be separate people. This practice, which is known as 'sock puppetting',[15] is discouraged by most sites which host discussions because it can be used to manipulate others. Sock puppets can be used to create an impression that someone has a lot of support from other members, or to create conflict by setting up arguments between two or more personas controlled by the same person. Sock puppets can also be used to undermine the smooth running of the boards by creating the impression that a member who argues with a moderator's ruling is supported by other members. If the use of sock puppets is uncovered, it will almost certainly upset people who were deceived. Many forums explicitly forbid sock puppets and will ban someone who is found to have been using them.

Christian leaders and experts

People sometimes claim they have offline credentials which give them extra status within the group. In a Christian context, this may take the form of claiming to be a church leader or an expert on spiritual matters. Even though it is widely known that 'ordinations' can be bought online, most people will not question the status of someone who calls him or herself 'Reverend' in an online context, just as they would not question the status of someone they saw wearing a clerical collar offline. Anyone with genuine ministerial status or an expertise in spiritual matters should be able to give details of his or her training and deployment that can be checked, and should not be offended to be asked.

Occasionally people who genuinely do have leadership roles in the wider Church will assume that this automatically gives them a leadership position in an online Christian group. Unless this has been offered on the basis of their commitment to the group and the qualities they bring to it, it should not be automatically assumed, any more than it would be assumed that a leader of one church has an automatic leadership position in any other church he or she goes into. If people believe they have an automatic right to be a member of the leadership team, it can be difficult to assert that they do not, because they may feel offended by what seems to be a rejection. However, it is a bad mistake to include anyone in the team simply because that person wants a role and feels entitled to it. Prospective team members need to demonstrate the emotional resilience and commitment to deal with the challenges that online ministry requires before they are asked to join the team.

Munchausen's by internet

In Munchausen's syndrome, those affected simulate the symptoms of serious illness, often taking drugs or injuring themselves in some way, because they crave attention. A related condition, Munchausen's by proxy, leads parents to simulate symptoms of serious illness in their children, apparently because they enjoy the attention that being the parent of a seriously ill child creates. It has been suggested that another, related disorder exists whereby people take advantage of online support groups by creating fake personas with dramatic problems. This form of impersonation has been labelled 'Munchausen's by internet'.[16] Online Christian communities which have been deceived in this way can be devastated when they discover prayer and support has been offered to someone who was essentially a fiction.

Such hoaxes are usually very elaborately staged. The false personas are given an online presence using online photo albums, social networking pages, websites and even 'friends' who join the group with them (who usually turn out to be sock puppets created by the same person).

In the paper 'Virtual factitious disorders and Munchausen by proxy'[17] several examples of Munchausen's by internet are given which all came to light because various members of a forum compared notes and became suspicious. 'Patient 1' presented as a Catholic monk with a rare, rapidly progressing form of cancer and said that because of his monastic lifestyle he was unable to seek treatment. He discussed his condition with an email support group for cancer sufferers and their relatives, including the daily visits of his nurse. He was found out to be hoaxing because

> over time, the energy level suggested by the person's lengthy and frequent communications to the participants, combined with his remarkable longevity without treatment, created suspicion among several members. One of them confronted him and, in a private response to that member, the man confessed that he had fabricated the information about his illness and his vocation. He withdrew from the list.[18]

'Patient 2' was a member of the same group professing to be suffering from lung cancer and undergoing the same treatments as other members of the group. She sometimes posted as her husband or one of her daughters. On one occasion, the 'daughter' posted detailed descriptions of a 12-hour operation her mother was meant to be undergoing, saying that her father, who was present at the hospital, was phoning her with updates as he received them from the surgical staff. Eventually, the hoax was uncovered, since

> as in patient 1, undeniable inconsistencies in the woman's story began to emerge, as did factual errors about the cancer treatment. These observations, combined with notable similarities in the writing styles of the woman and her various 'family members' led to a confrontation, like that described in the case of patient 1. She, too, promptly left the group.[19]

'Patient 3' joined a group dealing with chronic fatigue syndrome. She also posed as her friends and family members, and at times she used different internet accounts to sign in simultaneously as different people who often argued among themselves and distracted attention away from other group members who needed support. At one point, patient 3 said that her sister-in-law had 'committed suicide in despair' because she had not received enough support from group members. Although patient 3 initially attracted a great deal of sympathy and support, eventually

> several members began to recognize that such dramatic and exotic claims came continually from this person, that they seemed to increase when other members' reports were mobilizing nurturance, and much of the content was transparently false.[20]

In addition to the content appearing inauthentic, there were also linguistic clues about what was happening as a few people noticed that the posting styles of patient 3 and her relatives were very similar.

Unlike patients 1 and 2, patient 3 did not admit to the deception when confronted:

she alternately evaded the questions, denied the behaviour, or accused others. She, the 'husband', and the 'friend' subsequently stopped posting to this particular newsgroup, all at the same time.[21]

In this case, not everyone in the group believed that patient 3 was not genuine, and to prevent conflict among members about the issue the moderator imposed a ban on discussing the matter.

The authors of the paper report that the effects of these hoaxes on group members were in some cases severe:

> Patients 1 and 2, for instance, had a profound effect on the newsgroup subscribers, a reaction exacerbated by an episode in the same group in which a member had masqueraded as a physician. Some members became globally suspicious and started accusing others of deception, sending hostile missives (called 'flaming' in internet vernacular). Others expressed feelings of shame and hurt about having been duped or discussed their anger at the perpetrators of the ruses, each of whom had exited shortly after the falsehoods were discovered. In the case of patient 3, conflict among the woman's supporters and detractors led the moderator to ban the topic from discussion.[22]

It is assumed that those who display symptoms of Munchausen's syndrome and Munchausen's by proxy are disordered, because they do things that risk causing genuine harm to themselves or (in the case of Munchausen's by proxy) to others. People who perpetrate Munchausen's by internet hoaxes certainly seem to be seeking attention, and in a way that requires them to create a very intricate deception. However, since there seems to be little risk to the perpetrator other than the risk of being found out, it is far from clear that he or she is ill. There is, however, a clear risk of damage to the victims of such a hoax. As well as the feelings of suspicion, anger and hurt described above, there have been cases where monetary fraud has been committed, such as money raised for the funeral of someone who never existed, or donations for treatment that isn't needed.

Although most recorded cases of Munchausen's by internet take place in support groups for illnesses, online Christian groups do occasionally attract people who are pretending to have a health or social problem in order to elicit sympathy and support. While people often believe deceit to be widespread on the internet, within an online community it is often easier to pick up deception than it is offline. It is worth noting that patients 1, 2 and 3 were all detected as hoaxers by group members noticing discrepancies and comparing notes. Most people unintentionally give away more information that they think when they are posting online, even if they are trying to create a false persona, and if a discrepancy is suspected it is relatively easy to check back on what has been posted before. I have seen several hoaxers on Christian sites who have been found out by their own inability to present a story without mistakes. In one case, different people (both, it turned out, personas created by the hoaxer) posted an identical picture of 'their' cat.

As indicated in the case studies above, once you are fairly sure that there is some deceit involved, the best approach is to ask the person in private for an explanation. There are three common reactions – to admit it and apologize, to admit there has been some deception but claim that parts of the story are true, or to become very angry at the accusation, possibly making threats of legal or other retaliation. Whatever the initial reaction, if there is a hoax, the hoaxer will probably disappear quite soon after being approached. If the person will not admit to the hoax and continues posting, you will have to make a decision about whether to ban him or her to avoid further deception. It will probably be necessary to tell the community what has been discovered. People may be upset and angry at first, particularly if they have been actively involved in supporting the hoaxer. However, in all the cases I have seen on Christian sites, the anger has turned to forgiveness quite quickly.

This chapter has presented some of the extremes of bad behaviour you may encounter online, but it should not be assumed that this is commonplace. Most of the people I deal with online are a very positive influence in my life, but wherever two or three are gathered together, difficulties can arise, and relationships online are no different from relationships offline in that respect. Fortunately, extreme cases of bad behaviour are very rare, and we need to expect the best of people while being aware that, just occasionally, some people may let us down. This possibility reminds us that, online and offline, we should be both as innocent as doves *and* as wise as serpents.

7

Building an online community

---·•·•·•---

Even if your vision is for a project run solely by yourself, it is worth thinking about community. The online world is full of abandoned Christian sites, sadly forsaken and clogged up with adverts and spam posts which say nothing about the Christian mission they were created to promote. A better foundation and the support of a team can enable a project to grow beyond the vision and energy of its founder.

What do we mean by community?

A community is a group of people who have things in common, relating to each other through shared aims, interests or values. It is structured to be self-sustaining, so that when members leave the community continues. Community is intrinsic to Christianity – not only did Jesus work within a community of disciples, but the Christian faith was spread by the formation of communities which retold the stories of Jesus' ministry and brought other people to Christ through his presence in their midst. The nature of the Holy Trinity is a holy mystery, but it is arguable that there are elements of community within it.

It can be argued that it is only through community that Christianity can be observed and learned; the difference between creating a website for people to find out about Christianity and an online community where people can experience Christian community could be likened to the difference between giving someone a copy of the Highway Code to learn about driving and offering to take him or her out in your car to practise.

The word 'community' is often used very loosely, both on-line and offline, to mean a collection of people with a shared interest, but the sort of community we need to aim at for mission and ministry needs to be more self-sustaining and purposeful than that. Church leaders and well-known Christians who make themselves available online by blogging or on social networking sites often attract large numbers of followers who are referred to as a community, but such a group rarely takes on a life of its own. Once the individual stops interacting with group members, there is nothing left to hold it together and it dissipates.

Social networking sites enable people to connect with each other through shared acquaintances rather than shared interests or activities. As the name implies, the aim is simply to form networks through mutual acquaintances. Like the groups that gather round blogs, people who are brought together by mutual acquaintances aren't a true community because there are no shared values or aims that identify them as a group. A community requires boundaries, whereas networking operates across and through boundaries.

There may appear to be an exception around online activism – sometimes known as 'clicktivism' because it often centres around signing online letters and petitions – when people use their social networks to gather support for their causes. When there is a lot of interest in a particular issue, an online group may form on a social networking site to provide information about the campaign or cause that is being sup-ported and to encourage others to join. This may have the appearance of a community while the issue is current and members are keen to discuss the issue central to the group's formation. Single-issue groups rarely result in a long-term online community being formed because they are usually short term. Once the short-term aim of raising awareness has been met, its members will lose interest in visiting the group, which will gradually become inactive.

How do online communities form?

It shouldn't be possible for communities to form online. A conservative definition of 'community' always describes some kind of face-to-face interaction. But over the last century, sociologists have begun to observe different kinds of communities: those that are untethered from in-person contact. Sharing a physical space is no longer a prerequisite for feelings of belonging.[1]

In her book *Untangling the Web*, Aleks Krotoski describes seeing communities forming around online gaming. Once people have finished gaming together, they stay online to chat, finding out more about each other as people and developing personal links which form them into a non-intentional community – a community which was not foreseen or planned for by the game's creators.

Keith Stuart, a regular gamer, sees community as intrinsic to gaming:

> The history of the games industry is, ironically, not about industry in a lot of ways – it is about community ... The early era of mainframe computers also brought us the multi-user dungeon, text-only multiplayer adventure games that spread across university and research centre networks in the eighties. Pioneers like Richard Bartle and Will Crowther created online fantasy realms, which could be explored by groups of people who had never met in real-life, who may have been thousands of miles apart, but yet were able to help each other on imagined escapades.[2]

To him, the purpose of the game while it is being played is secondary to the sense of community that it creates among people who are meeting virtually by playing it.

While Krotoski has observed the creation of community among gamers, her intuition is that this is not only unexpected but in some way wrong. Her feeling is that 'It shouldn't be possible for communities to form online.' Objections to online Christian communities are often phrased in a similar way, reflecting a perception which is accepted as a self-evident truth that relationships are about being together, and 'being together', by definition, can only happen when we are in physical proximity to one another.

This perception is underpinned by what we know about how we relate to other people. When we are with someone in the same space we use body language, expression, clothes, accent and a plethora of other signs and signals, some of them subliminal, to inform ourselves about each other. None of this information is available to us when we are conversing online – we have to rely on what people explicitly tell us (and perhaps what they don't tell us) to get to know them. One of the biggest fears people express about online relationships is the potential for deceit – yet still, as Aleks Krotoski witnesses, people feel they are able to know enough about each other to form relationships and to develop a sense of belonging to a community. Krotoski describes how community is formed online:

> What happens online is weirdly like offline social life. There are community rules and regulations. People develop a strong sense of belonging that can influence what they do and what they think offline. There are cool groups and ones that you don't want to be associated with. And these groups, these communities, are anything but short term. There are some groups of strangers who have known each other online for over twenty years.[3]

A sign of a developing community is when members start to be interested in each other's lives and wellbeing as a group, celebrating birthdays and special events, sharing each other's joys and sorrows and asking for and receiving advice and support. Interactive online communities often arrange offline meetings (usually known as 'meets') between members who are geographically close or willing to travel.

An example of a community gathering around a website is the Ship of Fools.[4] Founded originally as a print magazine, which closed in 1983, Ship of Fools re-emerged as the online 'magazine of Christian unrest' on 1 April 1998, focusing on the often unintentional humour of religious life. The emergence of an interactive community among readers of the site was unexpected, as co-founder Simon Jenkins explained in an interview in American Christian satire magazine *The Door* in 2000:

> Yes, a major feature of the site is our discussion board, Ship-talk, which has taken on a life of its own and become a virtual community, complete with discussion, arguments, jokes, people traveling to meet each other, and a handful of people falling in love with each other. In fact, a good number of our British shipmates get together regularly for 'crew meets', which usually take place in English pubs over a large number of pints of beer. This is the really unexpected thing. When we started, we thought we were just launching a magazine – but we've found that we actually launched a community, too.[5]

If we identify online Christian communities as important to God's mission, we need to form community intentionally rather than accidentally, and structure it for mission and ministry. Each community will be different but it is helpful to consider whether there are steps we can take at the start which will make it easier to build a functional and self sustaining community.

Structuring the community

If we are seeking to establish Christian communities, it is sensible to see what the experience of other Christians can teach us. While the idea of the Christian faith being shared via the internet is relatively new, the idea of belonging to an unseen community is older. The 'communion of saints' mentioned in the Apostles' Creed is understood to mean the whole of the Church throughout space and time, and the 'cloud of witnesses' that we are told surrounds us in Hebrews 12.1 is made up of the martyrs (witnesses) of the Church who have gone before us. St Paul's letters were written as part of a continuing ministry of encouragement and oversight to the churches which he had founded and could not visit physically.

A holy temple in the Lord

When it comes to setting up an online community, it is often the virtual infrastructure that it is going to inhabit – the website, blogging site or virtual world artefact – that consumes the resources of time, money and attention.

However, as St Paul reminds us in his letter to the Ephesian church, in building a Christian community the materials we need to pay the most attention to are human and spiritual. We ourselves become part of the structure whose foundation is the saints and prophets who have gone before us. Jesus Christ is the essential cornerstone which keeps us together as 'a dwelling-place for God'.

> So then you are no longer strangers and aliens, but you are citizens with the saints and also members of the household of God, built upon the foundation of the apostles and prophets, with Christ Jesus himself as the cornerstone. In him the whole structure is joined together and grows into a holy temple in the Lord; in whom you also are built together spiritually into a dwelling-place for God.   (Ephesians 2.19–22)

The foundation of your project therefore needs not to be setting up a good-looking website but determining what your aims are and making sure you are setting out to build the right thing – a living structure within which people can see God at work.

Putting together an online project also needs to be done in the right sequence so that there is an underlying stability. As St Paul indicates in his words to the Ephesian church, Christian communities, like buildings, need a frame resting on firm foundations if they are going to be sufficiently strong and resilient to withstand the pressures and difficulties of ministering in Christ's name and being part of God's mission. Our foundation is to be the wisdom and example of the apostles and prophets we have received through the Bible and with whom we are joined through Christ. The framework for the community is its members, and Jesus is the cornerstone – the first stone which is put into the structure to guide the placement of all the other stones so that the building is straight.

While we may take the local church as the default model for Christian community, there are of course other kinds of community to draw on as examples, both ancient and contemporary.

Monasticism

When Jesus withdrew to the desert to fast and pray, he was following an accepted path for spiritual enlightenment which had also been followed by his cousin John (known as the Baptist) and the prophets Elijah and Elisha. The word 'monastic' has its roots in the Greek *monastikos*, meaning to live alone, and those who went to the desert lived a solitary (eremitic) life of prayer and fasting. Monastic communities formed and developed alongside the church as places of worship, ministry and mission, keeping alive ancient traditions of prayer. Those following the monastic life were seen as separate from the world, living apart in cloistered communities and only visible when serving in professions such as teaching and medicine which were part of their vocation.

In recent years, Christians have started to explore their tradition, rediscovering monastic rhythms of prayer which express our desire to connect with the roots of our faith – and with God – in ways which fit into our complex lives and allow us to reflect on and reduce their complexity. This provides a contrast not only to contemporary lifestyles but perhaps also to the social and administrative responsibilities that active membership of a local church may bring. The attractions of monasticism extend beyond practising Christians. Documentaries by the BBC, such as *The Monastery* and *The Monastery Revisited* in 2005–6 and *The Big Silence* in 2010, attracted huge audiences and many thousands of enquiries to Worth Abbey and St Beuno's retreat centre, where they were filmed. Volunteers were put into a monastic setting and asked to observe the disciplines of the community; they themselves were observed as they responded to it.

The growth of interest in monasticism has led many people to adopt monastic practices such as contemplative prayer and Ignatian meditation into their everyday lives. This in turn has led to the creation of non-residential communities such as the Moot Community in London, mayBe in Oxford and the Northumbria Community, which are often described as 'new monasticism'. The sense of community among dispersed members is fostered by following a common rule of life. Many Christians who are not members of new monastic communities build practices such as retreats and spiritual direction into their lives, reflecting the eremitic monastic tradition. They adhere to core monastic values and practices within their daily lives rather than withdrawing to a desert. Some people become oblates of monastic orders such as the Benedictines, following the rule of life of the order but living outside it.

Benedict of Nursia (*c.* 480–547) was the founder of the Benedictine order and his Rule for running monastic communities is still read today. After studying his faith for many years, and spending time as a hermit, Benedict was invited to became the abbot of a monastic community. He left when the monks tried to poison him. This experience led him to think about how a community could be formed and sustained. He put these thoughts into practice when a small community formed around him, writing them down in a series of daily readings which became known as the Rule of Benedict. Benedict's Rule emphasizes values such as listening, hospitality and simplicity, and has attracted interest in the last few years as a resource for businesses and other secular organizations who are seeking to improve the ethos of the workplace. This contemporary enthusiasm for the Rule sits oddly with the content of the daily readings, which sometimes advocate harsh punishments to enforce the Rule.

Monasticism relates to online community in several ways. The solitary nature of the monastic experience, which is lived out away from the rest of the world and partly in silence, resonates with the experience of online relationships, which require people to withdraw at least partially from the world around them to enter the virtual community via a computer or mobile device. The online community is often run without many of the chores that absorb members of the offline church, and so can focus more on the spiritual experiences which are being shared. Online communication is often conducted through writing, which slows down the pace and encourages listening.

Online communities are unlikely to accept the rulings of a powerful 'abbot' figure, but community members do need to agree about lines of accountability and how decisions are made. If the community members are the building blocks, clear lines of accountability and responsibilities are the mortar that helps them stay together.

Online communities are often set up with an idealistic belief that no arguments will arise since everyone shares the same vision and will readily agree on everything. The reality is that groups need to go through several stages of development before they become fully functional. The stages were identified by Bruce W. Tuckman in 1965 as 'forming, storming, norming and performing'.[6] Storming is an essential part of the group's development as a joint ethos and shared understanding of the group are developed, but if members are unable to deal with conflict productively the group will never move beyond this stage, disputes will be unresolved and decisions will be deferred, leaving the group unable to work together to fulfil its vision.

An online community which is stuck in the storming phase will find it hard to attract and keep members as it spends an increasing amount of time discussing how to manage itself, leaving little time and energy for mission and ministry.

Online communities as fresh expressions of church

The Church of England's publication in 2004 of *Mission-Shaped Church* – subtitled *Church planting and fresh expressions of church in a changing context* – introduced the phrase 'fresh expressions' as shorthand for a range of initiatives to bring the gospel to people who were not attracted by traditional forms of church.

In his foreword, the then Archbishop of Canterbury, Rowan Williams, wrote:

> we have begun to recognise there are many ways in which the reality of 'church' can exist. 'Church' as a map of territorial divisions (parishes and dioceses) is one – one that has a remarkable vigour in all sorts of contexts . . . But there are more and more others, of the kind this report describes and examines.[7]

At about the time *Mission-Shaped Church* was published, two separate 'internet churches' were set up: i-church was part of the Diocese of Oxford's Cutting Edge initiative, which encouraged the setting up of new, non-traditional forms of church and was initially funded by a grant from the Church of England, and the Church of Fools was set up as a three-month experiment with a grant from the Methodist Church of Great Britain. These were far from the first attempts to create Christian community online, but each of them had a 'hook' which caught the public imagination, with worldwide news stories creating a huge demand for access. The publicity for i-church hinged on the decision to advertise widely for the first 'web pastor' to be in charge of what was referred to as a 'virtual parish' for people who could not otherwise access church. The Church of Fools was a 3D virtual church in which users controlled avatars within an on-screen reconstruction of a Gothic church. Although arguments have raged about what constitutes 'proper church' since the publication of *Mission-Shaped Church*, resistance to the idea of online church as 'real church' was particularly strong, with most arguments hinging around the lack of sacraments and physical proximity to others in the congregation.

Rowan Williams' working definition of 'church' in his foreword to *Mission-Shaped Church* was broad and non-prescriptive:

> If 'church' is what happens when people encounter the Risen Jesus and commit themselves to sustaining and deepening that encounter in their encounter with each other, there is plenty of theological room for diversity of rhythm and style, so long as we have ways of identifying the same living Christ at the heart of every expression of Christian life in common. This immediately raises large questions about how different churches keep in contact and learn from each other, and about the kinds of leadership we need for this to happen.[8]

It is unlikely that Archbishop Rowan had virtual churches in mind when he wrote his definition of church, but the breadth of his vision of 'church' in the context of Fresh Expressions gives a way for online Christian communities to be viewed as part of the Church, and offers a methodology for setting up communities to fit new contexts which works as well online as offline.

The Fresh Expressions journey and online communities

The 'Fresh Expressions journey' is a description of how the groundwork for a new community appropriate to a specific context and culture often happens. The Fresh Expressions guide tells us that many fresh expressions of church:

- begin with a period of listening to God and to the people the missional team feels called to serve;

- develop by building loving relationships and through acts of service;
- create a sense of community in which evangelism can have its proper place;
- provide opportunities for individuals to explore becoming followers of Christ;
- encourage church to take shape around those entering faith.[9]

It is worth noticing that 'church' is not mentioned until all the other steps have been gone through, all of which are relational and service focused; so it is only at the last step – encourage church to take shape around those entering faith – that the question of whether 'church' can happen online needs to be considered. All the previous steps describe a process of discipleship which can clearly be undertaken through online relationships by those who have the particular gifts that are needed for forming online Christian community.

The vision for your online project will determine how you interpret the five steps towards forming community that are recommended for fresh expressions of church. However – as with the Benedictine Rule – listening to God and to others is of primary importance. It is important to think and pray hard about what group or groups you may be called to connect with before you make decisions about how you are going to develop your online presence. Remember that you are part of God's plan and not responsible for carrying out all of it. The aim is not to become the biggest online Christian community the world has ever seen, but to serve the people God is calling you to serve. How do you relate best to other people online? Can you develop relationships you've formed online in a non-Christian context, such as a support forum or a gaming site? Find others who share your vision to help you to discern what you are being called to do. Think about gathering a team to become the first community members and work out the vision with them.

How do we form community?

Membership of organizations offline is limited by factors like distance, cost and time commitments, but none of these are barriers to joining an online group. All online communities have a large fringe of members who are relatively inactive, and it is best to leave them at their preferred level of involvement rather than trying to chivvy them into joining in more. If you are looking to find more members for your community, it may seem obvious to try and convert some of these fringe members into more active membership, but this is rarely effective because you are trying to get them to do what you want and not what they want. We can have no idea of the effect we are having on people; some people may consider themselves part of your community without ever posting a word. It is a better use of time to find ways to connect with people who want to become active members right from the start.

Publicity can be a help in attracting new members, although it can also be counter-productive, as dealing with a large wave of new members with high expectations can be time-consuming and disheartening. Online Christian communities used to be considered a novelty, but it is unlikely that the formation of an online Christian community will ever again be a major news story worldwide. Any exposure in the mainstream media, especially on a national television or radio channel, will still attract a wave of new members, but many of them will probably disappear quite quickly, either because the site has not met their expectations or because they simply lose interest.

Having a page for your community on a social networking site such as Facebook enables members to involve their friends by inviting them to 'like' the page, posting links on their timelines and raising awareness. Be aware that social networking sites are not universally used, so if you focus your online presence exclusively on one of them you are excluding people who don't use that particular site. This is not necessarily a bad thing, but it does mean that people who are attracted by any form of publicity you are running may be unable to join your group if it is on a site they don't use. If you are developing a contextual ministry based around a particular social networking site, beware of becoming an evangelist for the site – work with the people who choose to spend time there rather than persuading your Christian friends to join the site so they can be part of your group.

Ending well

If people start to rely on your presence and you suddenly disappear, this can affect their view of the Church and even of God. If you are serious about using your project for evangelism, mission and discipleship, you need to think about sustainability right from the start.

However, there is another stage in the 'forming, storming, norming, performing' sequence – and that is adjourning or mourning. Sometimes a group needs to close, either because it is not working or growing as planned, or because it has simply fulfilled its aims and members need to be freed up to develop other ministries. If you do close the group, make sure that members know what is happening and have time to move on, and leave some indication of what has happened should people visit your website or page and expect to find you there.

The kingdom of God is like . . .

The kingdom parables in the Gospels compare the kingdom of God to a number of things – a mustard seed, a lost coin, a catch of fish, a hidden treasure . . . When I was turning over ideas for a sermon about the kingdom with a friend, I started wondering what signs of the kingdom we might look for online, and how our online communities might reflect that to others.

One of my strongest memories from my early days of online ministry is attending the closing service of the online church the Church of Fools, which was open for several months longer than originally planned but was too costly to keep open indefinitely. Steve Goddard, the co-founder of the Ship of Fools, preached on the first chapter of the letter to the Romans, including the passage:

> For I am longing to see you so that I may share with you some spiritual gift to strengthen you – or rather so that we may be mutually encouraged by each other's faith, both yours and mine. I want you to know, brothers and sisters, that I have often intended to come to you (but thus far have been prevented), in order that I may reap some harvest among you as I have among the rest of the Gentiles. I am a debtor both to Greeks and to barbarians, both to the wise and to the foolish – hence my eagerness to proclaim the gospel to you also who are in Rome.
>
> (Romans 1.11–15)

I did long to see these people, most of whom I had never met face to face and never would meet face to face, because we had prayed together, dealt with violent opposition and attempts to close us down together, worshipped together and tried to represent our faith by being there in that virtual church to represent Christ to real people we would never meet in the flesh.

Many of the parables of the kingdom involve persistence and the importance of small things to God. The community you form may be small. It may feel unimportant in the grand scheme of things. It may not attract hundreds of people and large amounts of publicity. But if the community reflects Christ's presence, then it will be bringing the kingdom.

8

Looking after yourself and your team

————◆•◆•◆————

Why is it that so many movements and organisations spring up within the Church and within society form a noble and generous purpose, attract intelligent and conscientious people, flourish briefly, then become so preoccupied with questions of internal organisation that their original purpose is forgotten, and they die?[1]

Most people who start a ministry are inspired by a vision of what they hope to achieve – they are focused on mission, both in the Christian sense of mission as making God known through their actions, and in the more secular sense of mission as the basic driving motivation for the organization's existence. Like the apostles at Pentecost, they may be on fire with the new idea that they have been inspired to bring into being. The excitement of starting something and getting it running will create more energy around a project. At this stage, tiredness and burnout are unlikely to pose a problem, but if the habit of running on adrenaline is acquired in the early days of a project it is hard to break later.

An online project can be started without many financial and human resources. It takes only one person to set up a website, arrange some publicity and wait for interested people to arrive. The first people to arrive will probably share the vision for online Christian mission, and a small number of enthusiasts can achieve an enormous amount if they share the same vision and the same goals. At this stage, there is little management to be done since decisions are made simply by a single person or by a small, like-minded team. This will change once you have created a resource that other people use and may come to rely on.

Human beings are infinitely creative, and once people become involved in your project they will change it. Problems will arise that you couldn't possibly have planned for, and new ideas that you would never have had on your own will start to emerge. While previously everyone was working to the same agenda, the need to negotiate about priorities and agree actions before taking them will develop. This can feel very irksome to those who have been involved from the beginning; people who have not invested the same time and effort as the pioneers of the project will start to express opinions, ask for an input into decision-making, and even complain.

At this point, the energy that envisioned and initiated the project can no longer be focused solely on developing it. There is also a need to find ways of maintaining the resources you have provided and the community that may have developed around them, while continuing to strive towards the vision which inspired you in the first place. Balancing these two modes of mission and maintenance within one organization can create tension, since people with a pioneering instinct are less likely to be energized by the work of maintaining what has been set up, while those who excel in maintaining what has been created may be unwilling to undergo any change in case it destroys what already exists. Things which have not previously needed any thought, such as how decisions are made, may start to be the focus of disputes and discontent, so that more and more time is taken up with running the community than with working towards the aims with which the community was set up.

This tendency to become more and more inwardly focused is not unique to online communities, but online communities have tools which make it very easy for them to slip into becoming consumed by the minutiae of their own existence. For example, an offline meeting has a beginning and an end, and will be held between people with a particular expertise or interest in the issues under discussion. In contrast, an online community may hold open-ended discussions on forums, encouraging everyone to have their say even if some are not particularly concerned about the issue under discussion. This can result in decisions being endlessly deferred, or the decision being made by default by whoever has the persistence and stamina to get the last word. Such processes can consume energy that should be spent on the primary purposes of the community. They may also become an arena for power struggles, where other disputes and grievances between members are played out. At this point, those with whom the vision originated may lose interest because of the difficulty of keeping the community on track and give way to a new leadership. This does not have to mean the end of a project – a change of leadership can bring a new vision for what has now emerged, and energy will again be generated by that vision. However, it may equally mean that the project has run its course and the purpose of the community is now to maintain the community, which will continue to exist more or less in its current form for as long as people have the enthusiasm to maintain it.

Burnout

The next day Moses sat as judge for the people, while the people stood around him from morning until evening. When Moses' father-in-law saw all that he was doing for the people, he said, 'What is this that you are doing for the people? Why do you sit alone, while all the people stand around you from morning until evening?' Moses said to his father-in-law, 'Because the people come to me to inquire of God. When they have a dispute, they come to me and I decide between one person and another, and I make known to them the statutes and instructions of God.' Moses' father-in-law said

*to him, 'What you are doing is not good. You will surely wear
yourself out, both you and these people with you. For the
task is too heavy for you; you cannot do it alone.'*

(*Exodus 18.13–18*)

We have all met people who are so pivotal to their organization that it is hard to imagine that it could continue to run
without them around. It is obvious that this is, in the long
term, bad for the indispensable person, bad for those he or she
works with and bad for the organization. Leaders need to lead
by example and create a culture in which knowledge is shared
and skills are learnt, so that the community has the collective
resources to continue beyond the involvement of those who
are most energetic at the start. This is healthy both for the
individuals involved and for the community they are part of.

The term 'burnout' was coined relatively recently by psycholo-
gist Herbert Freudenberger in his book *Burnout: The high cost
of high achievement*.[2] Burnout is the condition which results
when stress builds up in an individual to the point where it
affects the way that person functions, and is particularly associated with workplace stress. Burnout can result from unreasonable demands from managers and pressure to achieve them,
but it can also arise when the 'manager' making unreasonable
demands is our own perfectionism or need to be needed. In roles
where we are responsible for our own workload, a tendency to
perfectionism and overcommitment can be exploited by the
people for whom we feel responsible by asking us to take on
'just one more' thing that they want us to do. It is important
to remember that 'just one more' thing may be the straw that
breaks the camel's back, and that there is a strong theoretical
basis, known as catastrophe theory, for recognizing that adding
one more thing, however small, to a burden may make it liter-
ally unbearable.[3]

The passage from the book of Exodus, describing the intervention of Jethro, Moses' father-in-law, when he believes Moses

is doing too much, suggests that the risk of ministerial burn-out was known about long before the term was coined. Having achieved the mission he was given by God of leading the Israel-ites out of captivity, Moses now sets about the seemingly more mundane, but more complicated and long-term, task of creating a viable community. Jethro sees that Moses is taking far too much on his own shoulders and advises him to get help before he wears himself out.

In her book *Everyday God*,[4] Paula Gooder uses the example of Moses to reflect on the culture of workaholism which per-meates Christian organizations as much as secular ones. She observes:

> what begins as good quickly becomes destructive not only of ourselves but also of the people we are trying to care for. Whether this be on a large scale (such as Moses and the whole people of God) or on the small scale of our own friends and family, most is not best. Most is corrosive of our best selves and our best endeavours.[5]

It is therefore important for the wellbeing of the project, as well as ourselves, to make sure that we do not take on too much and risk becoming a liability rather than an asset. The project needs to be robust enough to run even if key people drop out through ill health, a change of priorities or simple loss of interest. In addition, each person brings his or her own unique gifts, skills and commitments to a community, and if there is no space for individuals to offer their gifts and talents this will limit what the community can achieve and become.

There are also spiritual dangers in believing you are vital to the project, even if you started it. What feels like service can easily become overcommitment. It is always a good idea to ask, before taking on another responsibility: first, 'Does this need doing?'; second, 'If so, do I need to be the person who does it?'; and third, 'What is the worst that can happen if this isn't done?'

Delegation

Since online community often involves a lot of interaction, it can be very demanding not just of time but of mental energy, with many different areas of responsibility to be thought about. If one person attempts to take sole responsibility for everything that happens, that person will soon become exhausted. Leadership does not mean leading every aspect of community life single-handedly but making sure that things happen. It is not possible for one person to meet every need that arises; different people will be able to offer relevant experience and knowledge which will strengthen the care and help that can be offered. Worship can be led by different people on different occasions, bringing a range of style and content. Prayer requests can be shared in a forum or small group.

When we are in charge of an area of work, we naturally carry it out in the way that suits us best; it can be hard to step back and allow someone else to do the work his or her own way, which may not suit us as well. It is particularly hard to give up tasks and areas of work that we ourselves find fulfilling, but it is very poor leadership to delegate only the tasks we don't enjoy doing ourselves. Not only do we deny people the opportunity to learn, by not involving others in decision-making and leadership we also create the community in our own image rather than reflecting the diversity that exists within it.

Conversely, it is important not to fall into the trap of giving away all the aspects of the work you find more enjoyable, while selflessly keeping for yourself the jobs you find the least rewarding and the most onerous to save other people from having to do them. Not only will this lead to boredom and stress on your own part, but you may be denying someone else the opportunity to shine. I learnt this when I was working as an administrator in the health service. I struggled for months with the task of transcribing and adding up rows and columns of figures to be submitted for national statistics on clinic attendance. This was before spreadsheets were in use, so figures had to be entered manually and added up on a calculator. I am not good with numbers and inevitably my columns would not add up properly and I'd have to go back to find out where I'd made a mistake. Eventually, because I needed the time for other jobs, I very apologetically asked a member of my team if she would be able to take it on. Her face lit up because she loved working with numbers, and she enjoyed the opportunity to sit down for a morning a week with the clinic attendance lists almost as much as I hated it!

Ideally, delegation should always be like this, with the task and the person so well matched that he or she is pleased to be asked to do it. When you are working with volunteers, delegating work to someone who is not enthusiastic about it is almost always going to result in it not being done very well or not being done at all. You need to look for those members of the community who are committed to its wellbeing and therefore willing to take on 'maintenance' tasks that have to be done for the community to function.

When you delegate an area of work to someone, be available to discuss it with him for as long as he needs to feel confident about taking it on, and be prepared to work with him for a short time until he is able to take sole responsibility. Once you have stepped back, don't step in again – provide a listening ear but be sparing with your advice unless it is asked for. Remember that you have asked your team member to do the job in his own way, not to replicate how you would have done it. Above all, be supportive if anything goes wrong and express your confidence that your team member is doing a good job despite the setback. The ability to reflect on what has gone wrong is a vital part of learning, and helping people to do this is an important part of delegation.

Building a team

Requests of emotional and spiritual support may be made to the leader more frequently than to anyone else, but people are often happy to be passed on to someone else appropriate for support once the initial request has been made. Those in leadership should always be looking for the gifts and skills other members bring to the community and be willing to support people while they develop them.

In order to be able to delegate, you will need to build a team of people who are committed to the project and are able to learn how to carry out different aspects of running the community and the website.

Some people may arrive in the community with existing experience of online Christian projects and/or technical expertise. While it is good to be able to draw on existing knowledge and expertise, sometimes people with previous experience will have a very firm idea about how an online community should function and will automatically try to impose this. There is the potential for a huge number of online Christian communities to form, each of them with its own unique style and calling, and it is important to discern how God wants to form the community you are in rather than simply copy another existing community.

There is also a danger that being open to suggestions can result in a 'client–provider' mentality, where community members make suggestions for things they might like to try out (e.g. a discussion forum on a particular topic or a particular style of worship) which the leadership then attempt to provide. The question 'Why don't we . . . ?' is very often a way of saying, 'Why don't *you* . . . ?' Any suggested new activity should always be assessed logistically before it is agreed to. Ask: Who is going to be responsible for it? What resources will it require? How long is it going to run? How many people are committed to participating if it goes ahead?

Sometimes people suggest activities because they lack the confidence to offer outright to take on the responsibility themselves. It can be helpful to contact someone and ask if she would consider leading the activity she has suggested herself. Someone who has a real vision for something new to happen within the community is the best person to take the idea forward, with support. Sometimes someone will be very enthusiastic about taking something on, but fail to deliver. This can happen to anyone, particularly if he or she has committed to something without thinking through the logistics. If you take such failures in your stride, team members will feel able to approach you sooner, rather than later, if they realize they are not going to be able to do what they have offered to do.

Preventing cliques and in-crowds from forming

It is usual for moderators and other team members to have access to private boards where they can discuss issues concerning these roles. Site administrators, forum moderators and chat room hosts may also have powers that others do not have, such as the ability to edit other people's posts as well as their own or to exclude people from the chat room. With additional privileges and private meeting space, the team can gradually move from being focused on serving the community into being a separate, inner community. Of course, there is nothing wrong with forming friendships with other people who are serving on the team, but if it becomes apparent that the team is operating as a clique it can create bad feeling among other community members, particularly if they believe they are being discussed behind their backs.

It is therefore wise to avoid discussion of community members unless it is strictly necessary. For example, if someone asks advice on how to deal with a particular community member who is causing difficulties, this can be given, but any extensive discussion of the community member beyond this should be avoided.

It is important that team members adhere to the letter and the spirit of any rules that are in force. I have seen several major arguments blow up on Christian sites when moderators or administrators seem to be exempt from rules that everyone else is following. At worst, enforcing rules that you yourself ignore is very divisive.

It is also important to make sure that additional powers such as access to private forums and editing abilities should be given only to those who need them to carry out a specific role, and should not be retained if the role is given up. This can sometimes be difficult – for example, when a long-standing team member steps down, it can feel odd not seeing that person on the team forum any more. However, if people retain powers and access that they don't need, the team will quickly take on the appearance of a clique, which will undermine the ethos of service.

Dealing with conflict

Conflict is a feature of many online communities, coming both from misunderstandings and from the fact that some people enjoy being argumentative. Resolving disputes – the area which Moses was attempting to take on without support – can be a frequent part of leadership in online communities. It can be very time-consuming and needs to be dealt with by a combination of community rules which seek to keep interaction positive and friendly, with disputes and arguments resolved fairly and quickly.

Hierarchical, top-down organizational structures don't work very well online since the medium equips us to share information and opinions very easily. Most online communities will start as small, informal networks, within which information can be shared and decisions made in a fairly ad hoc manner.

As your community grows numerically, it may become necessary to codify some basic agreements such as behaviour into lists of rules or expectations, so that these can be referred to at times of disagreement.

The best rules aren't a long list of 'dos and don'ts' to cover any possible situation, but an understandable set of expectations based on an agreed ethos. In Matthew's Gospel, Jesus sums up a code for living in two statements:

> He said to him, '"You shall love the Lord your God with all your heart, and with all your soul, and with all your mind." This is the greatest and first commandment. And a second is like it: "You shall love your neighbour as yourself." On these two commandments hang all the law and the prophets.'
>
> (Matthew 22.37–40)

People are usually asked to tick 'I agree' to the community rules when they join, but may not read what they say. However, the fact that the rules are there and people have signed up to them – even if they don't remember what is in them – can short-circuit many disagreements about behaviour.

Your list of rules may need to be slightly longer than the Summary of the Law but the principle of behaviour based on love of God and of others is one that can and should be adopted in a Christian community. While it is wise to avoid long lists of rules that try to cover any situation that might arise, you will need to give members specific guidance about what is expected of members of your community.[6] Rules themselves cannot change how people behave, but they can give an indication of what is and isn't acceptable, which can then be used to influence the behaviour of people whose conduct is problematic. Rules should therefore be as clear as possible about what is being asked and give no room for argument about what they mean. To avoid lengthy arguments, the rules themselves should make it clear who decides whether a rule has been broken.

Your rules should also state what sanctions can be applied. There are few sanctions that can be used in online communities other than temporary or permanent exclusion, and these should be used sparingly. Negotiation and persuasion are much more effective ways of moderating behaviour, especially if these come from other community members and not just the leadership. A short-term exclusion may defuse a conflict, but it may equally fuel more arguments if some members feel the exclusion is unfair. Permanent exclusion should only be used when it is clear that the person involved is unable to function as a member of the community and after warnings have been given. Signs that you should be considering permanent exclusion are if other members are being bullied or verbally abused by a member, if there is a repeated pattern of disruptive and destructive behaviour, or if the community's legal obligations are breached, e.g. if there is repeated posting of copyright material or potentially libellous statements.

Motivation and longevity

A sower went out to sow. And as he sowed, some seeds fell on the path, and the birds came and ate them up. Other seeds fell on rocky ground, where they did not have much soil, and they sprang up quickly, since they had no depth of soil. But when the sun rose, they were scorched; and since they had no root, they withered away. Other seeds fell among thorns, and the thorns grew up and choked them. Other seeds fell on good soil and brought forth grain, some a hundredfold, some sixty, some thirty.

(Matthew 13.3–8)

As Christians, we seek to be both culturally relevant, so we are heard by the people around us, and counter-cultural in challenging the assumptions and habits that take people further from God or prevent them from hearing the gospel.

The digital world is built for speed. It is possible to have an idea for an online campaign or initiative and set it up within weeks, if not days. If your project is unusual, or you have someone with a high profile involved, it is possible to gain a large amount of publicity very quickly. The downside of this is that things can disappear as quickly as they appear.

One approach to digital ministry is to go for high-speed, high-impact campaigns that have a short lifespan, arousing interest in the Christian message, hoping that people will be motivated to connect with a church that will take them on the next part of their Christian journey.

The counter-cultural strategy is to stay with our online ministry for the long haul, waiting for the seeds we are sowing to germinate and nurturing people in their Christian journey. This is a challenging and possibly a personally costly option. It may be possible to set up an online mega-church of millions of people, but it is more likely that a long-term online Christian community will be small and quiet rather than large and exciting, and may not be understood by the wider Church. As I said at the beginning of this book, the commonest question I am asked about online church is 'What do you do?' and it is hard to explain that we don't 'do' church – we are church to each other, despite the lack of sacraments or a building, because we are committed to each other's journeys in the faith and in Christ's love.

I have been conscious while I have been writing this book that it may sound rather daunting, with large amounts of space given to dealing with the more difficult aspects of online life. The downside of online mission and ministry is no greater than the downside of anything we undertake for God, but there is also a great sense of excitement and enjoyment in exploring a new form of ministry with others who are equally enthusiastic. Because the digital world moves so fast, one of the most striking statements we can make about the gospel and God's love is to be there for people and to remain there, praying, welcoming, teaching, comforting and being the good news for whoever needs us.

In the words of the visionary Mother Julian of Norwich, 'He did not say "You shall not be tempest-tossed, you shall not be work-weary, you shall not be discomforted." But he did say, "You shall not be overcome."'[7]

In the ever-changing digital world, what will not change is the person and nature of Jesus, his ministry of healing, his teaching of God's love and his death and resurrection. While we have those, we have nothing to fear.

Appendix 1

Example of a worship and prayer service for a chat room

Notes for leaders

If you are able to copy and paste the words into the chat room, the service will flow much more smoothly. If you are cutting and pasting, leave time for people to read each line before posting again.

To enable people to participate, give clear directions, e.g. 'Please join in by typing the words after the asterisk'; 'Please post a candle like this ['] when you have finished.'

If people come in after the start, type (Hello X) in brackets but don't restart the service as this just trains people to be late.

Make it clear when you have finished the service by posting a line of dashes or Xs.

x x x x x x x x x x x x x x x x x x x x x x x x x x x x x x x x

LEADER: As we bring our prayers to you,

ALL: *Hear what we ask you, O God.

LEADER: As we share in worship,

ALL: *Be among us, O God,

LEADER: Now and for ever,

ALL: *Amen.

(Wait until all have said 'Amen' before continuing.)

LEADER: Reading: Luke 4.1–13.

Jesus, full of the Holy Spirit, returned from the Jordan and was led by the Spirit in the wilderness, where for forty days he was tempted by the devil.

He ate nothing at all during those days, and when they were over, he was famished.

The devil said to him, 'If you are the Son of God, command this stone to become a loaf of bread.'

Jesus answered him, 'It is written, "One does not live by bread alone."' Then the devil led him up and showed him in an instant all the kingdoms of the world.

And the devil said to him, 'To you I will give their glory and all this authority; for it has been given over to me, and I give it to anyone I please. If you, then, will worship me, it will all be yours.'

Jesus answered him, 'It is written, "Worship the Lord your God, and serve only him."'

Then the devil took him to Jerusalem, and placed him on the pinnacle of the temple, saying to him, 'If you are the Son of God, throw yourself down from here, for it is written, "He will command his angels concerning you, to protect you", and "On their hands they will bear you up, so that you will not dash your foot against a stone."'

Jesus answered him, 'It is said, "Do not put the Lord your God to the test."' When the devil had finished every test, he departed from him until an opportune time.

This is the word of the Lord.

ALL: *Thanks be to God.

LEADER: We now offer our prayers for ourselves and others. Please type your prayers, or simply a candle ['] if you would rather not pray 'out loud'.

(Wait until there is a pause in the prayers before you continue.)

Appendix 1

LEADER: We now join our prayers together in the prayer that
          Jesus taught us, the Lord's Prayer. Please say it in
          your own time and in the version you prefer, typing
          'Amen' when you have finished.

(Wait for everyone to type 'Amen' before continuing.)

(Closing prayer)

LEADER: May Jesus be with each of us
          and those we love
          this night *(as appropriate)* and always,

ALL: *Amen.

Appendix 2
Sample forum rules

In order to make these boards a pleasant and safe place, we ask you to abide by some simple but important rules.

1 **Respect the person behind the screen.** Treat people as you would wish to be treated – with consideration and respect. Personal attacks are not allowed. If you are attacked, don't post in anger. Contact a host and ask him or her to deal with it.

2 **Respect people's time.** The people who post here (including hosts) have other responsibilities and real lives as well – don't expect instant responses.

3 **Respect the bandwidth.** These forums are free to use but they cost money to run, so use them for the purpose they are set up for. In particular, please note the following points:

   (a) Don't crusade (post about your favourite cause or topic regardless of the topic of the thread you're on).
   (b) Don't use the forums to conduct vendettas and feuds with individuals or organizations.
   (c) Don't advertise commercial products.
   (d) Don't post copyright or obscene material.
   (e) Don't post comments which could be seen as libellous or defamatory.

4 **Respect the hosts.** Hosts are here to keep the boards safe and enjoyable. If they ask you to do something, please do it. If you have a problem with the way a host has acted please contact one of the administrators.

5 **Respect yourself.** Swearing, txt spk and long rambling posts generally don't come across well. Make sure what you write is clear and concise and gives a good impression of you. Please do not allow anyone else to use your account to post – you are responsible for what is posted in your name.

6 **Respect your own and other people's privacy.** Some people don't mind being known by their real names, others keep their identity in real life private. If you know someone offline, or find out his or her offline identity, don't disclose it. Don't disclose your own or other people's contact details – you have no idea who might read them.

7 **Respect the Christian ethos of the site.** Members of all faiths and those with no faith are all welcome here, but remember we are a Christian site. If you don't want to read about Christianity or to hear how Christians think and feel, perhaps our forums are not for you.

8 **Respect our rules about identity.** Please be aware that the use of pseudonyms does not remove your responsibility for what you post. *Web User* magazine published legal guidelines for the internet which stated, 'If your target is identifiable and what you have written exposes them to "hatred, ridicule or contempt", hurts their reputation or causes them to be "shunned or avoided", you could end up in a civil court.' You cannot assume that a member is not identifiable simply because that person is using a pseudonym. In addition, please note you are only allowed one identity on this board – sock-puppetry is a serious breach of trust and will be treated as such.

9 **Research guidelines.** If you wish to conduct any sort of research on the site or with our members you must contact one of the administrators to seek permission and ask for guidance as to what is acceptable. Any posts regarding research will be removed if this has not been done.

10 **If in doubt, just ask.** If you need to change your user name for any reason, or need any other help or advice on using our websites, please contact an administrator.

11 **Forgive one another.** Remember we all make mistakes and we all upset other people at times. Arguments and feuds between posters make the forums unpleasant for everyone, so:

(a) if what you have said has upset someone, please apologize;

(b) if someone says sorry, please accept it;

(c) if you are asked to drop an argument, please drop it;

(d) if it's not your argument, please don't join in;

(e) if you want to conduct a feud with another member, please find somewhere else to do it.

Appendix 3
Further reading

Ori Brafman and Rod A. Beckstrom, *The Starfish and the Spider*, Harmondsworth: Penguin, 2007.

Douglas Estes, *SimChurch: Being the Church in the virtual world*, Grand Rapids, Michigan: Zondervan, 2009.

Aleks Krotoski, *Untangling the Web: What the internet is doing to you*, London: Faber and Faber, 2013.

Charles Leadbeater (and 257 other people), *We-Think: The power of mass creativity*, London: Profile Books, 2008.

Clay Shirky, *Here Comes Everybody: The power of organising without organisations*, London: Allen Lane, 2008.

Sue Thomas, *Technobiophilia: Nature and cyberspace*, London: Bloomsbury Academic, 2013.

Appendix 4
Useful websites

Christianity: <www.christianity.org.uk>
The CODEC Research Centre for Digital Theology: <www.dur.
   ac.uk/codec/>
i-church: <www.i-church.org>
Lifechurch TV: <http://live.lifechurch.tv>
Now a Christian: <www.nowachristian.org>
Partakers: <www.partakers.co.uk>
Rejesus: <www.rejesus.co.uk>
St Pixels: <www.stpixels.com>
Ship of Fools: <www.shipoffools.com>

Notes

Techno Christianity

1 <www.shipoffools.com>.

2 While some people fundamentally disagree that a group meeting online can be called a church, people who have started online missionary groups often have no hesitation in referring to their group as church. This points to some interesting differences of opinion about what 'church' really is, which are explored in Chapter 2.

3 The Church of Fools later became St Pixels, <www.stpixels.com>.

4 <www.i-church.com> was started by the Diocese of Oxford in 2004 at about the same time as the Church of Fools opened.

5 The *Oxford English Dictionary* dates the first use of the word 'technology' to the early seventeenth century, defining it as '1. The application of scientific knowledge for practical purposes, especially in industry: 1.2 Machinery and devices developed from scientific knowledge: 1.3 The branch of knowledge dealing with engineering or applied sciences'; <www.oxforddictionaries.com/definition/english/technology>.

6 Eric Schatzberg, 'Technik comes to America: changing meanings of technology before 1930', *Technology and Culture*, 47 (3), July 2006, pp. 486–512.

7 'A timeline of computer history', cataloguing exhibits in the Computer History Museum, can be found at <www.computerhistory.org/timeline/?category=cmptr>.

8 Intriguingly, the *Oxford English Dictionary* lists one meaning of 'information' as 'Chiefly in Christian Church: Divine influence or direction; inspiration, esp. through the Holy Spirit'; <www.oed.com/viewdictionaryentry/Entry/95568>.

9 Shane Hipps, *Flickering Pixels: How technology shapes your faith*, Grand Rapids, Michigan: Zondervan, 2009.

10 Hipps, *Flickering Pixels*, p. 24.

11 Hipps, *Flickering Pixels*, p. 25.
12 Hipps, *Flickering Pixels*, p. 48.
13 Hipps, *Flickering Pixels*, p. 48.

2 Theological understandings

1 Critical incident analysis (CIA) is a widely used reflective learning process in which the practitioner reflects on an event which made him or her stop and think – known as a 'significant event' – in order to understand his or her actions and learn from them for the future. This is done within a framework of questions to help the reflective learning process. For more information and a suggested framework see, for example, Melanie Parris, *An Introduction to Social Work Practice*, Milton Keynes: Open University Press, 2012, Element 2, 'Reflection and critical thinking', pp. 39–40.

2 An action learning set (ALS) is a small group reflective learning process where each person is given the space to think through an issue with the help of group members. A facilitator maintains boundaries and enables the group to focus on exploration rather than advice giving.

3 'What is the mixed economy?' from *Fresh Expressions: The Guide*, <www.freshexpressions.org.uk/guide/about/mixedeconomy>.

4 Brent Strawn, *Holes in the Tower of Babel*, Oxford Biblical Studies Online, <http://global.oup.com/obso/focus/focus_on_towerbabel/>, accessed 26 January 2014.

5 Jonny Baker, *The Network of Christ*, on his blog at: <http://jonnybaker.blogs.com/jonnybaker/2008/10/the-network-of.html>.

6 Douglas Estes, *SimChurch: Being the Church in the virtual world*, Grand Rapids, Michigan: Zondervan, 2009, p. 117.

7 Estes, *SimChurch*, p. 117.

8 Estes, *SimChurch*, pp. 119–20.

9 Amy McLeod, 'How did we get here?' 19 June 2011, Article vfutur.es/8qdgQ, <http://virtualfutures.co.uk/tag/skeuomorphism/>.

3 Where do I start?

1 This helpful advice came from Andrew Graystone, director of the Church and Media Network. Andrew has written and spoken extensively about his belief that using our own names is vital to

ensure humanity in our online relationships, e.g. in his article 'Credit where it's due', published on theMediaNet.org on 7 August 2013: <www.themedianet.org/article?article=37a12ee9-85fe-4f7c-9929-f9b164f1aa5f>.

2 Paula Gooder, *Everyday God*, Norwich: Canterbury Press, 2012, p. 59.

4 Pastoral care and relationships

1 Entry from John Wesley's Journal, 11 June 1739, cited at <http://en.wikiquote.org/wiki/John_Wesley>, accessed 23 July 2014.

2 e.g. Acts 4.32–35.

3 'Person hours' means the total of all the hours offered, e.g. three people offering five hours a week totals 15 person hours.

5 Online discipleship and spirituality

1 The phrase 'New Age' covers a range of philosophies, beliefs and practices, offering freedom to the individual to choose a spiritual pathway that makes sense to him or her. The interface between New Age and Christian beliefs as a basis for mission and evangelism is explored in Anne Richards, Steven Croft, Yvonne Richmond, Nick Spencer and Rob Frost, *Evangelism in a Spiritual Age: Communicating faith in a changing culture*, Norwich: Church House Publishing, 2005.

2 'God wants people to become disciples of Jesus', from *Fresh Expressions: The Guide*, <www.freshexpressions.org.uk/guide/about/principles/disciples>.

3 For example, the Methodist Church of Great Britain has introduced an initiative called Deepening Discipleship, and some Church of England dioceses, such as Canterbury and Hereford, are also developing Deepening Discipleship material. Liverpool Cathedral has a Canon for Discipleship, while the Fresh Expressions movement, in partnership with, among others, the Church of England, the Church of Scotland, the Methodist Church of Great Britain, the United Reformed Church and the Salvation Army, makes discipleship a key aim in growing new churches.

4 Acts 17.17.

5 There are in fact plenty of 'experts' online – theologically educated people who see their presence and engagement online as part of

their calling, and who are happy to participate in collaborative learning as well as more traditional methods of teaching and preaching.

6 Mark Easton, 'Prayers for Muamba', <www.bbc.co.uk/news/uk-17429779>.

7 Easton, 'Prayers for Muamba'.

8 Two churches which have offered live streaming in recent years are Luss Parish Church near Loch Lomond in the Church of Scotland and Deddington Parish Church in Oxfordshire in the Church of England.

9 In the Church of England, Communion by extension is when an authorized person takes bread and wine that have been blessed in a Communion service to someone who was not able to attend.

10 There is an example of an online worship service in Appendix 1 which you are free to use or adapt.

11 William A. Barry and William J. Connolly, *The Practice of Spiritual Direction*, Glasgow: A. & C. Black, 2003.

12 For a more detailed discussion of the qualities needed for spiritual direction, see Diane Reynolds' article on the website for the Liturgy Office of the Catholic Church of England and Wales, 'What are the qualities of a "good" spiritual director?' <www.liturgyoffice.org.uk/Prayer/Spirituality/Spiritual-Director.shtml>.

13 Abba Paphnutius, quoted in Margaret Guenther, *Holy Listening: The Art of Spiritual Direction*, Lanham, Maryland: Rowman and Littlefield, 1992.

14 The Retreat Association website is at <www.retreats.org.uk>; the London Spirituality Centre website is at <www.spiritualitycentre.org/>.

6 Dealing with difficult and disruptive people

1 See the *Daily Telegraph*, 'Twitter trolls admit abusing feminist campaigner online', 7 January 2014, <www.telegraph.co.uk/technology/twitter/10556507/Twitter-trolls-admit-abusing-feminist-campaigner-online.html>, and *The Independent*, 'Twitter "trolls" Isabella Sorley and John Nimmo jailed for abusing feminist campaigner Caroline Criado-Perez', 24 January 2014, <www.independent.co.uk/news/

uk/crime/twitter-trolls-isabella-sorley-and-john-nimmo-jailed-for-abusing-feminist-campaigner-caroline-criadoperez-9083829.html>.

2 Support of people who understand working online is absolutely vital for anyone starting or taking over an online ministry. Other people may simply not understand the intensity of the inter-actions you are experiencing.

3 See Chapter 8 for information about team selection and supervision.

4 It should not be assumed from this that all Christians necessarily behave well when they are online. Sometimes Christians use online Christian sites to 'vent' or 'act out' in ways that social convention forbids in an offline church.

5 Ronald L. Grimes, Ute Hüsken, Udo Simon and Eric Venbrux, *Ritual, Media and Conflict*, Oxford: Oxford University Press, 2011, p. 168.

6 An example of trolling behaviour would be to join a discussion group for supporters of the monarchy and post insulting comments about the Queen.

7 It is well known among forum administrators that threads on which people are arguing attract far more views than other threads.

8 If you find yourself in this situation, taking a break of a few days from going online usually sorts it out, since the aggressor will turn his or her attentions to someone else. If the aggression escalates into threats then it is worth a call to the police to check if any law is being broken.

9 George Simon, *In Sheep's Clothing: Understanding and dealing with manipulative people*, Marion, Michigan: Parkhurst Brothers, 2010, pp. 25–6.

10 Websites which successfully invite user contributions, such as Wikipedia, have very clear rules about what sort of material can be posted and enforce them by consistent moderation.

11 An example of forum rules can be found in Appendix 2.

12 Most forums will have T&Cs you can draw on to create your own, or see the example in Appendix 2.

13 It's important to realize that using a pseudonym or pseudonyms doesn't offer as much protection as people believe it does, since

email addresses, location of their broadband server and details people give about themselves when posting online mean that it can be possible to identify people who don't give their real names.

14 e.g. the blogger 'Archbishop Cranmer' who refers to himself as 'Cranmer' across different social media platforms and writes as if he is the sixteenth-century archbishop of that name.

15 A 'sock puppet' in American English is known as a 'glove puppet' in UK English – in both cases, the persona is being operated by someone else.

16 See, for example, the *Guardian* article by Jenny Kleeman, 'Sick note: faking illness online', 26 February 2011, <www.guardian.co.uk/lifeandstyle/2011/feb/26/faking-illness-online-munchausen>.

17 Marc D. Feldman, Maureen Bibby and Susan D. Crites, 'Virtual factitious disorders and Munchausen by proxy', *Western Journal of Medicine*, 168 (6), June 1998, pp. 537–9.

18 Feldman *et al.*, 'Virtual factitious disorders', pp. 537–8.

19 Feldman *et al.*, 'Virtual factitious disorders', p. 538.

20 Feldman *et al.*, 'Virtual factitious disorders', p. 538.

21 Feldman *et al.*, 'Virtual factitious disorders', p. 538.

22 Feldman *et al.*, 'Virtual factitious disorders', p. 538.

7 Building an online community

1 Aleks Krotoski, *Untangling the Web*, London: Faber and Faber, 2013, pp. 50–1.

2 Keith Stuart, 'Gamer communities: the positive side', *Guardian Games Blog*, 31 July 2013, <www.theguardian.com/technology/gamesblog/2013/jul/31/gamer-communities-positive-side-twitter>.

3 Krotoski, *Untangling the Web*, p. 50.

4 The Ship of Fools website can be found at <www.shipoffools.com>.

5 Simon Jenkins' interview with *Door* contributing editor Becky Garrison is reproduced on the Ship of Fools website: <www.ship-of-fools.com/shipstuff/story/door_interview.html>.

6 The original paper by B. W. Tuckman was 'Developmental sequence in small groups', *Psychological Bulletin*, 63 (6), 1965, pp. 384–99. Information about Tuckman's theory of group formation is readily available online.

7 Rowan Williams, Fr Damian Feeney SSC, George Lings, Chris Neal and Graham Cray, *Mission-Shaped Church*, Norwich: Church House Publishing, 2004, p. vii.

8 Williams *et al.*, *Mission-Shaped Church*, p. vii.

9 'How do fresh expressions develop?' from *Fresh Expressions: The Guide*, <www.freshexpressions.org.uk/guide/develop>.

8 Looking after yourself and your team

1 Gerard W. Hughes, *God of Surprises*, London: Darton, Longman and Todd, 1990 edition, p. 142.

2 Dr Herbert J. Freudenberger with Geraldine Richelson, *Burnout: The high cost of high achievement*, London: Anchor Books, 1980.

3 For a scholarly but readable account of catastrophe theory and stress, see Jack T. Tapp, 'Multisystems holistic model of health, stress and coping', in P. M. McCabe, N. Schneiderman and Tiffany M. Field (eds) *Stress and Coping, Volume 1*, Hove: Psychology Press, 1985; see p. 296, 'Catastrophe theory model of active coping and conservation-withdrawal'.

4 Paula Gooder, *Everyday God*, Norwich: Canterbury Press, 2012.

5 Gooder, *Everyday God*, pp. 43–4.

6 A sample set of forum rules can be seen in Appendix 2.

7 Julian of Norwich, *Revelations of Divine Love*, 22.

Did you know that SPCK is a registered charity?

As well as publishing great books by leading Christian authors, we also . . .

. . . **make assemblies meaningful and fun for over a million children** by running www.assemblies.org.uk, a popular website that provides free assembly scripts for teachers. For many children, school assembly is the only contact they have with Christian faith and culture, and the only time in their week for spiritual reflection.

. . . **help prisoners become confident readers** with our easy-to-read stories. Poor literacy is a huge barrier to rehabilitation. Prisoners identify with the believable heroes of our gritty fiction, but questions at the end of each chapter help them to examine their choices from a moral perspective and to build their reading confidence.

. . . **support student ministers overseas in their training**. We give them free, specially written theology books, the International Study Guides. These books really do make a difference, not just to students but to ministers and, through them, to a whole community.

Please support these great schemes: visit www.spck.org.uk/support-us to find out more.